Best wishes

Gene Kathmans

I Was There, Charley

An Autobiography

By

Clemens A. Kathman

S/Sgt. 200th Coast Artillery (AA)

Illustrated

authorHOUSE™

1663 LIBERTY DRIVE, SUITE 200
BLOOMINGTON, INDIANA 47403
(800) 839-8640
WWW.AUTHORHOUSE.COM

© 2005 Clemens A. Kathman. All Rights Reserved.

No part of this book may be reproduced, stored in a retrieval system, or transmitted by any means without the written permission of the author.

First published by AuthorHouse 01/19/05

ISBN: 1-4208-1481-8 (sc)
ISBN: 1-4208-1482-6 (dj)

Printed in the United States of America
Bloomington, Indiana

This book is printed on acid-free paper.

"To endure the unendurable is true endurance"

Japanese Proverb

DEDICATION

In memory of Captain Sidney Seid, MD, 19th Bomb group, USAF and medical doctor in the Japanese Prisoner of War camp at Hirohata Japan. I owe him my life. To the many, many brave and courageous men of Bataan and Corriegdor who did or did not live to return to their loved ones. To my parents (now long deceased) who lived in painful suspense for three and a half years, not knowing the fate of their eldest child. To my first wife, LaVerne of forty-two years (also deceased) for putting up with me through the early years of our marriage while I was learning to act human again. To my second wife, Mary (deceased), who encouraged me to start this project. Lastly, I will be forever grateful to my present wife, Margaret who lovingly coaxed, cajoled, edited and helped me complete the task. To all of these beautiful people I humbly dedicate this book—cak--

ABOUT THE AUTHOR

The author, Clemens A. Kathman, 88 (better know as Clem), is a product of the "great depression", who worked his way through college, only to have Hitler, Mussolini and Tojo foul up his best laid plans. He was drafted March 1941, assigned to 200th CA(AA). December 8, 1941, the Japanese bombed Clark Field and he was in a shooting war. Bataan, the Death March and 3 1/2 years as a POW, he was liberated in September 1945.

Fourteen months hospitalized, he received his discharge, married and resumed his work in the newspaper field to see the transition from hot type printing to digital and photo-composition. Clem retired in 1981 and lost his first wife to emphysema and a second to heart and lung disease. 1992 to 2002 it was bachelorhood and the Masonic fraternity. He met his present wife on the internet and they were married in July 2002. They live in Brenham, Texas. Both dabble in writing. This is his first book.

TABLE OF CONTENTS

PREFACE XI

CHAPTER ONE EARLY DAYS IN THE ARMY MARCH 19, 1941--DECEMBER 8, 1941 1

CHAPTER TWO BATAAN AND THE DEATH MARCH 12

CHAPTER THREE O'DONNELL, HELL-HOLE OF CREATION APRIL 12, 1942--JUNE 1, 1942 40

CHAPTER FOUR CABANATUAN JUNE 2, 1942 -- SEPT. 18, 1943 60

CHAPTER FIVE HIROHATA, JAPAN SEPTEMBER 3, 1943-- JUNE 19, 1945 86

CHAPTER SIX FUSIKI CAMP JUNE 23, 1945--SEPTEMBER 5, 1945 128

CHAPTER SEVEN WE ARE GOING HOME SEPT, 5--30, 1945 157

CHAPTER EIGHT BACK TO THE HOSPITAL FEBRUARY, 1946--JUNE, 1947 191

EPILOGUE 198

PREFACE

Since retiring from the United States Army in July of 1946 I have intended, and have been urged by family and friends, to write about my six plus years in the army and more especially the three and half year spent in a Japanese prisoner of war camp. I started this endeavor shortly after being discharged while working for some college friends who were getting started in the printing business. Thanks to their encouragement and that of others, I began to try relating the many horrors, brutality, starvation, sickness and death associated with that experience. The first months I worked at it quite feverishly, but as time went on, the attempts at writing took a back seat. I was newly married, had new employment and was generally getting into the groove. Due to the diversion of everyday existence, pursuing the termination of this book faded into the background and it has only been in the past few years, at the urging of my children and grandchildren, that I have "picked up the old pen" and am going on with the book I started some 50 years ago. This book, or portions of it will be included in my autobiography, which is being written only for family and a few close friends. It would probably be dull reading to any one but the family.

I have copious notes and from September 1943 until January 1945, a diary written (against rules) on my allotted roll of paper-thin toilet paper, a copy of which is shown at the end of this Preface. I've used these notes to open the portals of my 88 year-old mind and hopefully, produce a document that is interesting, informative, sometimes controversial, mind-boggling, brutally frank and often amusing. The subject matter contained within is not altogether pleasant, and just writing about it, can never convey to the reader the inhumanity and depravity that the captives of the Japanese were exposed to, nor the traumatic effect it had on me and the many other young men who received this treatment by a supposed civilized nation. I can only relate what I saw and experienced. Many books have been written on this subject over the years, and I do not know that mine will be so different. I only know this is something I set out to do a long time ago and now am doing it, not just for myself, but to give voice to those unfortunate others who lived through this hell on earth with me. Thanks for your time, and for listening.

The Author in 1941

CHAPTER ONE
EARLY DAYS IN THE ARMY MARCH 19, 1941--DECEMBER 8, 1941

Shortly after finishing school at Texas Technological University in the spring of 1940, the U.S. Government passed and put into effect the Selective Service Act due to the chaotic conditions developing in Europe. I drew a very small number out of the fishbowl lottery. I was A-1 and a prime subject for the draft. It would have been almost impossible to find anyone willing to hire me for a permanent job, so I prepared myself for the inevitable draft notice. Meanwhile, I did freelance, writing sports for some of the daily newspapers in eastern New Mexico and West Texas. My notice came March 18, 1941. Before being bussed to Santa Fe, New Mexico, the 31 draftees were exposed to a very dull but supposed patriotic speech by the newly appointed head of the local draft board. He was as new to the job as we were and I'm sure he got better as the years wore on. We all took it with a grain of salt and prepared for a new experience that most of our fathers had encountered a few years before during WWI.

At the time, we believed we were in for only a year, but that was a pipe dream. The one year extended into years and years more, and the most humiliating part of it was that we were not in service to our country, but rotting in a stinking Japanese POW camp. But that is neither here nor there. If we had known what the future held, many of us would have ended it all before even embarking upon our life struggle.

One could write profusely just about the many odd, different and strange thing a rookie is subject to his first few day just to get in this man's army. If you were, like I was, a small town country boy, you had never in your wildest dream, imagined what you had to go though just to get in the Army.

We embarked by bus to Santa Fe. This being somewhat of a special occasion, (where they found it, being a dry county), many of the new draftees were pretty loaded when they were "poured on the bus." Upon arriving in Santa Fe we were bedded in for the night and urine tests were taken. There being some 70 plus of us from different parts of the state, I wonder what percent of the urine tests were alcohol. This was not a big factor, for those fellows were the first ones to pass the next day when we were either accepted or rejected. Of the 75, only three failed to make the grade and were sent back to their respective counties and, no doubt, rated 4-F.

After being sworn in and made a part of Uncle Sam's army, we received another patriotic speech, loaded on buses and taken to Albuquerque to board the train for El Paso, under the wings of a regular Army Sergeant we all thought was an officer. Anyway he gave that appearance to a bunch of green rookies on their way to where and what, was anyone's guess.

It was my fortunate or unfortunate luck to be appointed acting Corporal on the trip to the Reception Center, depending on the way you look at it. As it turned out it was a first class headache. The Sergeant turned in early and I was told to see that the guys got to bed early. Well, you can imagine one civilian telling another civilian what to do. Especially since they had not been in the army long enough to have even the faintest idea of what military discipline entailed. Mentally we were still civilians and civilians don't like to be told what to do. So rather that incur the wrath of the 70 plus civilian rookie, I did not see them drinking or playing poker. Either my luck panned out or the Sergeant was a sound sleeper. We arrived in El Paso early the next morning no worse for the activities.

The Reception Center at Ft Bliss, like all the early army camps that mushroomed after the Selective Service Act was passed, was life in the raw. It consisted of a few rough buildings thrown together to house the Quartermaster offices and warehouses, P. X. Chapel, Mess Halls, Latrines and Officer's quarters. The remainder of the camp was made up of pyramid tents mounted on a wooden platform and boarded up about three feet on the sides, with an opening on one side to access the tent. In the middle of he tent sat a gas heater to keep the tent warm during cold weather. Six steel army cots with mattresses were positioned around the perimeter of the inside and a 25-watt light bulb suspended from the center of the tent was the only light source. During warmer weather and summer the flaps of the tent could be rolled up for ventilation. The floor was rough hewn lumber that you were not sure would withstand the traffic of the many boots that stomped across it.

Immediately upon arrival we were assigned to a tent and afterwards marched to the Quartermaster supply to be issued mattresses, blankets, sheets, pillows and pillowcases and taught how to make a bed according to the U. S. Army. Now there is a way to do most everything. There is "The right way, and the wrong way" and there is the "Army way." In learning how to make up a bed the "Army way" was the first of many tasks where this rule applied. At least we had a place to sleep, which, as it turned out, was not all that bad. To this day I make the bed the Army way.

The first day in the Reception Center we were questioned, interrogated, tested, fed and issued. We gave our life history down to how many times we had dandruff or athlete's foot. We were interrogated as to what we had done and what we would like to do in this man's army. Then we were given I.Q. tests which would stop Dr. I.Q. of Kay Keyser. (quiz shows featured on radio in the late 30s and early 40s). In between tests etc. we went through a line and were vaccinated for smallpox and given shots for typhoid fever, after which we were measured for clothes and fitted for shoes. As usual in the army, they came in two sizes, too big or too small.

Lunch was an ordeal. Given mess kits earlier in the morning, we got in a line almost two blocks long where we stood for nearly an hour, received chow only to be rushed through eating it, then back for more skull practice. This time we listened to the Articles of War. It was my opinion these laws existed so officers could lord it over lowly enlisted personnel. We went in looking for the worst, and found it.

This, plus a few other minor formations, terminated the afternoon's repertoire. We retired to our respective tents worn out, down-in-the-mouth, lonesome and to top it off, it started raining. Listening to the rain falling gloomily on the tent, there likely was not one of the 70 plus men not trying to think of a way out.

After a good night's sleep, a sunny morning and a hot breakfast, we felt better about the whole deal. There wasn't much on that morning but stick around our respective tents and wait for the other shoe to drop. Charles Puttoff, a watchmaker friend of mine who was inducted with me, was called in earlier in the morning. He returned to get his gear and tell me he was being shipped out. The Air Corps was badly in need of Instrument Technicians and they were sending him to an Elgin Air Field in Illinois. He was my last link to home, but I bade him goodbye. That was the last time I ever saw him and I still do not know what happened to him.

There was a rumor floating around that some of us were to be shipped out that afternoon. I suppose that was the first rumor that I heard in the Army, but it was not to be the last. I may write a story on rumors, their cause and effect, but I doubt that I could remember enough of them now to make it worthwhile. Rumors or not, 50 of us were called out about three that afternoon. Rumors had us going to the east coast, the west coast and even Panama. To our own surprise, when we loaded into trucks, we rode about a half mile up the highway to the Anti-Air Craft Training Center situated on the side of Franklin Mountains and assigned to the 200th Coast Artillery (the New Mexico National Guard Unit) that had been nationalized in January 1941. It was Saturday and we were given temporary lodging until Monday, when we would be given our permanent battery assignment.

The 200th CAC was not at full strength, so the army brass was bringing it up to full strength by assigning draftees from New Mexico to the regiment. The guard was made up basically of kids from 18 to 25 who, during the depression and aftermath, joined the National Guard to augment any paltry income they were getting. Most of the draftees were older and more worldly-wise. We had one thing common, we were all native New Mexicans and were to realize the importance of that heritage later on.

I Was There, Charley

The first three weeks in the Army were just short of pure hell, or so I thought. Up at 6 a.m., fifteen minutes of strenuous exercise, breakfast, police call, then the remainder of the morning doing close-order drills in the sun and wind and rocks. If you have lived in that part of Texas and Eastern New Mexico, you know the horrible weather in February, March and April. Up and down, back and forth we marched over a newly constructed drill field that had been cleared off the side of a mountain. Try walking over gravel and rock, up hill and down under the best conditions, then imagine trying to do it and keep in step at the same time, doing a right or left pivot, all under the tutelage of a young kid, his ego swelled to the breaking point because of a couple of stripes on his shirt sleeve. For grown, mature men in their twenties who had been supervising employees for years, his was an irritant that grated on the ego to no small extent. Again we were dreaming at night of a way out. All of us had started counting the days until our year was up.

The afternoon was very little different. Instead of marching we sat out in the wind and listened to lectures on 50 and 30 caliber machine guns, how to field strip them and put them back together again. There was poison gas drills in which you learned how to put on and take off a gas mask, in the presence of gas. We learned how to drive all types of vehicles used by the army. We learned all about our rifle, about first aid in the field, and a thousand other things that I never realized was so important to being a soldier. When the day was over we could go to the P. X., drink a beer or two, play a game of ping-pong and then be in bed by the time the bugle blew taps. Another day, another dollar was a big laugh. On our first payday, we drew twenty-one dollars and were told that we would get that for the next three paydays. It wasn't until the fifth monthly payday that we started getting the old dollar a day, thirty dollars a month.

The first 13 weeks constituted basic training. By this time, a recruit should be proficient in the basics of being a soldier. The 13 weeks was pretty general for all men drafted into any branch of the service. From there he went into training in whatever specialty he was assigned. Anti-Craft being our branch of the service, we would be in the Searchlight, three-inch gun, 37 mm gun, or 50-caliber machine gun batteries. I ended up in Battery H, a 37-mm gun outfit. Here again a choice had to be made. Was it guns, communication, or tracking The gun crews had already been picked by the old guardsmen, so that left the communication and tracking units to be filled by recruits. I chose communication because I had training in radio and electronics, but I learned all communication was done by field telephones with batteries and magnet ringers on them. Real primitive, but that was where we were in 1941. In my third month, our Battery commander went to gunnery school at Ft. Monmouth and a Lt. Parker from B Battery was sent over to fill his place. At this time, equipment was finally received and General Sage issued an order that all table of organizations should. be filled. Lt. Parker gave exams to those who desired to be non-commissioned officers, to check their proficiency to be non-coms. I took the test and secured a Corporal rating in the Communication section, which at that time, made me a twenty-one dollar Corporal for a month until my four months were up.

This, I think, was the turning point of my Army career. I no longer hated the Army. I had a job and responsibility. I began enjoying my duties, feeling as all good soldiers should feel...that my regiment was the best in the Army, my battalion was he best in the regiment, my battery the best in the battalion, my squad the best in the battery and I, the best damn soldier in the whole dad-burned army.

The summer of 1941 was a series of overnight maneuvers, hikes, convoys here and there, drills, more lectures and plenty of hard work to harden us for actual combat duty. This was the one thing we did not like to think about, but with the world condition in the shape it was at that time it was hard not to see the handwriting on the wall. In July, while other units of the Army were fighting mosquitoes down on Louisiana maneuvers, we heard rumors we would be joining them. In fact, some of our truck drivers were sent down to drive trucks and sweat out the heat and mosquitoes.

It was about this time that the Air Corps lowered their requirements for pilot training and opened an enlistment office at Beaumont Hospital in Ft Bliss to give physical examinations. I had taken the examination at Texas Tech in the spring of 1940 just before I graduated, but failed because of high blood pressure. I obtained permission from the battery commander for a days' leave to take the exam. A week or 10 days later, I received a letter to report to the Dallas Aeronautical School at Love Field in Dallas in September. The battery commander would not grant me a transfer out at that time because it was only a letter and not Army orders. I waited for orders to come down until we shipped overseas in August, but they never did. Later, at Clark Field in the Philippines, I received a follow-up order to report to Clark Field for another exam, later getting orders to report back on the first available transport, which was January 8 1942. The rest is history as I lived it, and am relating it in this book.

About the first part of August 1941, orders came down to prepare for maneuvers. The 1st Cavalry division had been in Ft. Bliss on maneuvers and we had set up in battle position in conjunction with them a couple of times. Now we were to maneuver on our own, but it was to be a pleasant form of simulating combat. We were on a good will tour of New Mexico, visiting several towns which headquartered the batteries making up the 200th CAC. Little did we know that would be the last time we would see that state or our families and friends for a long, long time. Had we have known then the situation we were getting ourselves in, the unit would have been several men short when it got back to Ft. Bliss, but we didn't know at that time we would be shipping out within the next two weeks. Oh, I imagine the brass knew, but probably wouldn't admit it.

The trip was a huge success in more ways than one. We got some actual experience in convoy maneuvers, making and breaking camp, setting up for action in unfamiliar territory, living in adverse conditions such as rain, hail and mud, all of which was to come in handy later on. Many of us saw parts of the state we had never seen before. Many were able to visit parents, wives and children as we passed through and spent the night at their respective home towns, Las Cruces, Silver City, Deming, Hot Springs, Belen, Albuquerque, Vaughn, Roswell, Artesia, Carlsbad, Ruidoso, Carrizoso, Almagordo and back to El Paso. In most all of the places, entertainment and refreshments were prepared for us. We, in turn, did our part of entertaining and informing the people of what made the Army tick, so we were in a very jubilant mood when we returned to Ft. Bliss where we received word we would be shipping overseas about the end of the month. (August 1941) Then the meaning of the "good will" tour became clear to us.

A week after orders were received, the 1st Battalion shipped out by train for San Francisco and from there, we could only guess. Rumors had us going to Alaska, Canal Zone and elsewhere. Ten days later the 2nd Battalion entrained for San Francisco, August 31, 1941, and three days later we were on Angel Island at Ft. McDowell, out in the middle of San Francisco Bay.

We were only there long enough to get the necessary shots, physical check ups, and check in our woolen OD uniforms. This meant we were going somewhere where it wasn't cold. We were given a short half day to visit San Francisco before we shipped out the next day. We boarded the SS President Coolidge, the "Queen of the Pacific" liner that regularly made trips to the orient. It had been partially converted to a troop ship with bunks set up in the freight holes and the promenade deck. A few of the amenities still remained for the convenience of Americans being evacuated from the many Pacific places being in the path of the advancing Japanese. Staterooms, where the officers were assigned, as well as the big lounge in the fore part of the ship, and the main dining hall, library, tearoom and orchestra, still remained for use. Battery H was situated on the Promenade deck right outside the large lounge. We slept in four tiered rows of bunks and enjoyed all he luxuries afforded the officers in the lounge, namely, free movies, concerts etc. Compared to later troop ships, we had just about all the luxuries one could imagine on a first class liner. The first two days I didn't much care whether I lived or died because of seasickness, but after that, the trip wasn't bad. Just monotonous, boring and long, 18 days.

Honolulu was a disappointment because we had such a short time to see it. We docked at 8 a.m. for supplies and to let some first class passengers off, mostly officers stationed in Hawaii. We were allowed to go ashore, but had to be back aboard by 4:30 p.m., which gave us only about six hours to see the sights. About all I remember of Honolulu is Waikiki Beach and my disappointment of it and the Royal Hawaiian Hotel. Having seen it featured on newsreels and movies it was a far cry from what I had in mind, but I did enjoy the visit to the Dole Pineapple grounds. Then we were off again for 14 long, hot and boring days. In spite of the luxuries of the ship, the same thing day in and out gets terribly monotonous. Therefore, it was a happy day when we pulled into Manila harbor. Having passed many small islands for a day or more we knew it wasn't going to be too much longer. It was time to get my feet on solid ground. Water is alright for drinking and bathing, but too much goes a long way.

Manila was very different from anything I had imagined. I don't know exactly what I expected to see, but I do know that I was somewhat disappointed. Instead of bamboo huts, ox-carts and things tropical, we stepped off the Coolidge into what appeared to be some Southern California seaport. Taxis and buses were screaming and honking, news boys were hawking the afternoon edition of the evening paper, the sea front was adorned with beautiful buildings, homes and hotels surrounded by lush green lawns and palm trees. Wide paved streets that cut their way through the business district resembled any American city. Many other striking counterparts reminded us of the land we had left only a short time ago.

It wasn't until we had boarded some dilapidated buses (not the one we had seen running along the dock) and reached the outskirts of Manila on out way to Ft. Stotsenberg, some 90 kilometers due north, that we saw the Philippines we expected to see. Wide open spaces, wallowing in rice paddies and surrounded or dotted by bamboo groves, diminutive natives dressed in denims either working the paddies or driving carabao carts or calesas (small pony carts) along narrow dirt roads. Barrios of Nipa palm and bamboo shacks heaped together ever few miles along the highway. Little brown-skinned youngsters darted along the road to curiously stare at us as we passed, and it started raining in Manila as only it can rain during the wet season in the tropics. At last we were here. "The front door to the Orient." Every way we looked, every breath we took, every sound that entered our ears told us so.

We arrived at Ft Stotsenberg in the middle of the night, too late to do much but flake out on the floor of the yet, unseen sawali barracks we had been thrust into. Come morning, a warm breakfast, and cots were issued along with sheets, mattresses, mosquito net, pillows and other equipment to make our domicile comfortable. Later our footlockers were brought in and we were ready to set up housekeeping.

Up until this time we had taken our life and its meaning lightly. Europe was in turmoil and every day looked as if we would be in it next, but so far we had taken it as a matter of fact that we would do our year in the Army and then back home. Even when we got orders that we were sailing to the Philippines, I thought that if we got into an affair with Hitler we would be in the safest place in the world. I was so sure that our trouble was with the Nazis, that the Japanese were the last ones to be troublemakers.

This idea changed fast. We hadn't been in the Philippines a week until we realized the hot box we had been dumped into. How naive I was. In the states, I did not realize the nearness of the Japanese or the eminent danger to which our little protectorate in the Far East was being subjected. It didn't take long to find out. Pick up a newspaper, listen to the radio, or just talk to one of the natives and you couldn't help finding out that the Rising Sun was directing its rays on those little islands. In fact, we were greeted as more or less liberators to both the native Filipino and what few troops the U. S. already had in the islands. The first thing they told us was the islands needed more and still more troops if they were to hold off an invasion by the Japanese. We laughed at them. We couldn't see it. But only a few days later it began to dawn loud and clear. Where there is smoke, there has to be a fire. We were beginning to see smoke in the form of high-flying reconnaissance planes flying over the islands. By the middle of November, we were moved into field position with the daily alert of high-flying planes.

It was not much of a surprise after being in the field for two weeks, early on the morning of December 8, 1941, to receive the news of Pearl Harbor and shortly thereafter, feel the mighty blow from 54 Japanese bombers as they dropped their loads on Clark Field, and the next forty-five minutes being the target of dive bombers and strafing zeros making like mosquitoes as they peppered us at will. This was war and there was not a doubt about it among the some twenty-four hundred 200th CAC men and officers. We were in a shooting war and as Sherman said "It was hell."

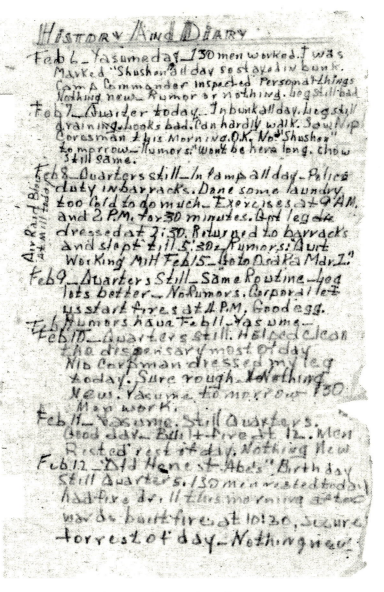

Example page from diary

CHAPTER TWO
BATAAN AND THE DEATH MARCH

In the few months since arriving in the Philippines until the Japanese hit Clark Field December 8, 1941, we'd made the most of the little time in the islands. The first few weeks were spent getting our Nipa barracks in order. Since the camp had just been started, we were pretty crowded until completion of all the barracks. It rained most every afternoon until dry season set in. Duty was light in the tropics. After a short turn of duty from 7 a.m. to 11:30 a.m. we were off the remainder of the day. Some of the batteries did have a little skull knocking after lunch for updating instructions, an area where we were weak. After 2 p.m. it was do pretty much do as you please.

A lot of time was spent in sight seeing. The Philippines are a very colorful group of tropical islands and lends itself to photography bugs. The P. X. Theatre on the Ft. Stotsenberg premises offered matinee and nighttime movies. I saw "Gone With The Wind" for the third time while there. The P. X. offered most anything you could get stateside and at quite a saving. Being somewhat of a camera bug, I had stored my camera equipment when I was inducted into the service; however, I was able to purchase some quality equipment from the P. X. and several of the camera hacks had started building a dark room next to the latrine to develop our film and make pictures. It was never finished, as the fiasco December 8, 1941 at Clark Field brought our project to a screeching halt.

Weekend passes were available to Manila and Baguio, a resort center in the mountains of northern Luzon, which catered to mostly officers and tourists. Most of the men who were not photo addicts were content to spend their off hours in the enlisted men's club at Clark Field, lapping up San Miguel beer or Los Angeles, a small barrio about three or four miles down the highway from Clark Field. I have been using Ft. Stotsenberg and Clark Field interchangeable, so I might take time here to explain that they are one and the same. Ft.

Sotsenberg is an old Army post dating from the Spanish-American War, in the advent of airplanes in warfare. Clark Field was carved out of the fertile plains adjoining Ft Stotsenberg. Clark Field was the home of 40 P-40 fighters, 20 B-17 long range bombers, 2 B-18 lighter bombers and other miscellaneous aircraft. Ft. Stotsenberg was the base for the 26th Cavalry regiment (Filipino Scouts), the 86th and 88th Field Artillery (Filipino Scouts made up of Filipino enlisted personnel and non-commissioned officers with U. S. Army officers), Quartermaster and Signal Corp, the 200th Coast Artillery (AA), 194th Tank Battalion, 192nd Tank Battalion, and 17th Ordnance Company, The latter three arriving in the Philippines after October 1, 1941.

Los Angeles was one of few places enlisted men could get off the post and visit or do sight seeing, find good eating (mostly friend chicken), drinking and dancing. It was an escape, and most of us took advantage of the facilities it offered.

After the first week of November, life at Ft. Stotsenberg took on an air of tenseness and apprehension. The previous months had been spent in preparation and maneuvers, now it appeared we might actually be forced to use this intensive training. We moved into field position around Clark Field and were on 24-hour watch. This meant we lived, slept, and ate in our gun positions a half mile north of Clark Field. The only men left in camp were the cooks who brought hot food to our position in trucks three times a day.

Action came as we had expected but sooner than we had anticipated. On the morning of December 8, 1941, having the sleep barely rubbed from our eyes, we were shocked by the news of the brutal and cowardly attack on Pearl Harbor by the Japanese Navy Air Force. It was not that they had struck, we half expected it, but it was the location they had attacked that astounded us as well as the rest of the world.

We had hardly recovered from news of the Pearl Attack, when about 12:30 p.m., listening to Don Bell, the Walter Winchell of Manila, we heard the warning to the Philippines of the impending dangers and heard him rapping the government for not doing anything about it. Bell had done a hitch or two in the orient with the 4th Marine Regiment, after which he had been doing radio news reporting in the Philippines. We thought with his background in the orient, he should pretty well know what was going on. He had just completed his noon broadcast about the Pearl Harbor attack and its significance, warning that the Japanese' next point of attack would be Clark Field.

I don't suppose he had signed off more that five minutes when we heard a loud drone coming from north of our position. Naturally, we looked that way and immediately caught the sun's reflection from a group of small dots high, high in the sky.

On the telephone, I connected to the Battery control post and heard someone say there were 54 of 'em. The 268s (forerunner of radar) were used to pin- point the plane at night so the searchlight batteries could determine accurately any number up into the thousands. I relayed this to our platoon commander and heard one guy say it must be our navy, but another declared them to be Jap. His buddy asserted that it couldn't be Japanese because they couldn't fly formation that good. It didn't make much difference who they were, they were coming too fast.

Formation, good or bad, the next thing we heard was a whistling noise and a loud explosion like a thousand shotguns going off at once. The whole ground shook under our feet. Looking south to Clark Field we saw a mass of billowing smoke, dust and fire. We had been bombed and although it was our first time, no one had to tell us what had happened.

The next 45 minutes were the most hectic I ever expect to go through. Up until that time we had "don't fire unless your are fired upon" orders. Now we had been slapped and it was time to fight back as best we knew how. The big 3-inch ack-ack guns opened up and were soon placing high explosive too close for the comfort of Mr. Jap. The high-flying bombers broke formation and two or three were seen trailing smoke as they beat a hasty retreat. They had done their job and good, but the worst was yet to come.

It was only the beginning. As the "big boys" faded away into the blue, dive-bombers and Zeros based on a carrier of the coast of northern Luzon swarmed in upon us. The action really heated up. Heretofore, the heavy bombers, flying so high, were out of range of the 37 mm anti-aircraft and 50-caliber guns, now, as the smaller and low-flying aircraft appeared, our work was cut out for us. We opened up with everything from 45 automatic pistols to the 37 mm guns. It was hardly an orderly affair, but then first experiences ever are as we expect them to be.

Being non-com in charge of the communication squad, I was completely left out of the firing order. During the excitement every one that was not on one of the 37 mm gun crews picked up their rifles and started firing at the nearest "flaming asshole", the big red dot on the low-flying planes, insignia for the Japanese rising sun. I was no exception. Sometime during the melee I heard the buzzer on the telephone go off. I looked around to see who was manning the phone. No one! A fine bunch of men I had in my squad, but, what the heck, I was no better. So, dodging between swinging rifle barrels in that small dugout, I managed to make my way to the buzzing phone, clamp the earpiece to my ear to hear the first sergeant ask the platoon for a checkup.

Taking a glance through smoke and dust kicked up by the two 37s, I did not see anyone down and every one was accounted for. I reported the same back to the sergeant and found out our third and fourth platoons were not so lucky. The Zeros had been strafing back and forth, left and right at anything they saw moving. The two platoons were situated north and east of Clark Field in an area of sugarcane and cogon grass. The tracer bullets from the strafing Zero set fire to the cogon grass and cane, completely burning them out. Several men were severely burned and were being taken to the hospital at Ft Stotsenberg and later to Sternberg Hospital in Manila. It was then that I really became aware of just what had really happened. Up until then it had felt good just firing at the planes and trying to get even, now the thought I could get killed hit me like a bolt out of the blue and I got that very empty feeling right in the middle of my gut.

I don't know if I was scared or mad or both at what I had just heard. Forgetting the phone, I grabbed up my rifle and started throwing clip after clip of ammo at those Zeros as they circled over our gun position to make another strafing run. The barrel of the rifle was so hot if it had not been for the wooden part, my hand would have been badly burned. One Zero, hit by 37 mm fire, crashed and burned in the cane field a short distance from our gun position.

Suddenly, it was over. Just as fast as it started. I came out of the dugout and almost fell on my face. I felt as weak as a kitten. I sat down on an ammo box and took a long drag from my canteen. My other squad members joined me and everyone was trying to talk at once. Nervousness? Fatigue? Hyper? Who knows. By the time the chow truck arrived that evening most of us were taking on an appearance of normality, yet when I put that first bite of food to mouth, I would have upchucked if there had been anything there. I was sick. I mean sick. Lt. Ashby asked why I wasn't eating and when I told him my trouble he went over to his bedroll and took out a bottle of orange gin and told me to take a big swig. Dubiously, I raised the bottle and took a swig. It burned going down, but in a few minutes I was hungry and ate my meal. For the next few days, the good Lieutenant shared his bottle of orange gin. From then on I ate anything that did not eat me first.

A quick checkup of our platoon showed that no one was seriously injured. Herschal Grooms had received a fragment from a steel water drum that had been hit when one of the 37 mm gun barrels was lowed too far and sent a high explosive projectile into it. "Was only a scratch" was the injured reply. Two men of Battery E were killed as they were taking chow to their gun position. Several air corps personnel lost their lives due to their close proximity to the airfield. Many more were injured. We later buried an Air Corp pilot who had driven his car into a cane patch and was strafed to death. Of the 36 B-17s lined up on the field, 7 were completely destroyed. Others received damages but were later repaired and flown out to Australia. The pursuit squadron had been moved to Nichols Field near Manila shortly before the raid and escaped.

I Was There, Charley

The Japanese had done a beautiful job of destroying the surrounding areas, but had only stirred up the wrath of all concerned. Not that there was a lot we could do about it, except sit and wait. Ours was a defensive outfit, not offensive. That was a feeling I will never, ever forget. I think most everyone else felt the same way. We were scared, angry, sick all wrapped in one. Chastised for no reason other than the ego of a power hungry dictator. Insulted for the cowardly way they went about it. I shall forever despise the Japanese for their sneaking, cowardly ways. I can't help but think, in spite of the fact that they are our ally today, that given the same situation again, history would repeat itself.

Shortly after the raid, orders came down from Regimental Headquarters that the whole regiment would be split in half to form another anti-craft outfit with the newly arrived equipment sitting on the dock in Manila. . Half of the regiment left that night to pick up the new equipment and the 515th CAC became a new fighting unit in the field. This reduced the number of men to man the equipment and guns but would put twice the firepower into action. This meant that we were going to have to put the old proverbial shoulder to the wheel and do the best we could.

As if the thought of being at war was not enough, this order had us reeling. Imagine the big decision our platoon commander, Jack Ashby, had to make. Dividing a close-knit unit was just like breaking up a family. In a way, we were a family, having worked so hard and diligently for the past 10 months. We had become a polished team any way you split it. Some close buddies would now be separated. I stayed with the 200th, but lost three of my best men to the newly formed 515th. On top of that, they sent my truck driver to a half-track outfit. Lt. Ashby stayed with the 200th but was later transferred to Headquarters G-2.

This division left H Battery, 200th CAC with exactly 15 men to man two guns, range section, and communication. When my truck driver was transferred, that left me with just two men and me to man the telephones 24 hours day, but I could have not asked for two better men: General Shelton from Boonesville, Arkansas and Robert J. Moore from Conroe, Texas. We did away with the range section altogether because it was too slow to track the Zeros. We just tried to figure their flight route and throw up a barrage fire and hope they ran into it. Most of our equipment was obsolete…it was pitiful, but we made do with what we had. The two men relieved from tracking section were placed on the gun crew and helped man the phones in a pinch. You really had to be versatile in that army.

The Japanese lost little time in following up their first raid. The next few days were a series of raids on Clark Field by dive-bombers and Zeros. By the end of the week, we heard they had made landing at Lingayan Gulf on the most northern part of the island. Runway repair crews were repairing craters at Clark Field as fast as the Japanese bombers were destroying it. Hot Anti-aircraft fire diverted their bomb runs so that only an occasional bomb actually hit the runways, but the cane fields surrounding the airfield really caught it. B-17s were still able to take off and were doing what damage they could to delay the landing. It was on one of those raids that Capt. Colin Kelly lost is life in a valiant flight sinking a Japanese warship. His flight crew had bailed out just before reaching Clark Field and we were unfortunate enough to have to watch as the Japanese Zeros viciously strafed them as they were helplessly suspended from their parachutes on the way down. A few survived to relate information of the heroics.

The day after the tragic loss of Captain Kelly and his plane, we began to notice the smell of rotting flesh. It seemed to be coming from the area where the Zero had crashed and burned. During a lull in action, Sgt. Ragadale, Pfc. Moore and myself chose to investigate. We found where it had gone down. Except for a wing that had been thrown clear, it had completely burned. We found the pilot, or what was left of him, minus legs, head and arms. A foot, still in a shoe, was a short distance from the burned sight. The most ironic part of the investigation was in finding what appeared to be a generator with the nameplate of a well-known American manufacturer stamped on it.

For the first couple of weeks we were well informed of the war both to the North and to the South. The Japanese had landed at Lingayan in the north and Legaspi on the Batangas peninsula in the south driving up toward Manila as reported by Don Bell in his vitriolic attack on the Japanese and the attack on the Philippines, but as the days wore on we did not need the radio to tell us the news. The thunder of the field artillery of both side, getting louder meant just one thing. They were getting too close for comfort.

Christmas eve night, shortly after the chow truck had made its evening rounds, orders to evacuate came down from regimental headquarters. We were to destroy anything we could not take with us. We made a quick trip to the barrack area to empty what we could from our footlocker into our barracks bags. The footlockers and their remains we buried in the fields adjoining our gun position I don't think there was a one of us who really thought we would be digging them up again. Ever. We loaded everything in the two, 2-1/2-ton trucks that were pulling the two 37 mm guns, lined up in the convoy awaiting orders to move out.

"March Order" came about 10:30 that night and started us out on one of the most hectic nights imaginable. Traveling 45 miles per hour, driving a 'right side of the road' vehicle on the left side of the road, blacked out, in convoy with the enemy supposedly hot on your tail, can get pretty hairy. Sometime during the night, the kitchen truck tried to straddle a concrete road marker and ripped the whole underside out. The cargo was spread out over the other vehicles, including our two. Heretofore, I had managed to doze some, but now with a frozen side of beef as a bed partner, sleep was out of the question.

Besides running off the road a couple of times and a few bumper bang –ups, we pulled into a cane patch near the little town of Hermosa some where west and south of Manila on the road into the Bataan peninsula, Early Christmas day. Our objective here was to furnish anti-aircraft protection to keep the Jap airplanes from bombing the bridge the troops withdrawing into Bataan had to cross. 'Bataan, the land of our last stand.' Poetic! No?

It was Christmas Day. What irony. A day of peace on earth, good will toward men. What peace? Good will? Bah, humbug. I thought. Yea, war is no respecter of Sunday and Holidays. Most of the day was spent in digging foxholes, setting up and trying to camouflage our gun position. That was a joke. We had two air raids in the afternoon. The best they could do was bomb a small nipa hut at least a hundred yards from the bridge

Instead of turkey, cranberry sauce and all the trimmings of Christmas, we had to content ourselves with a can of C-rations and biscuits for lunch. That evening the cooks excelled themselves in spite of the conditions under which they had to work. My frozen bed partner became a beautiful piece of roast beef, accompanied with gravy and the usual trimmings. Anything warm would have been welcome, but this was a feast.

After we had finished out banquets, three or four of us retired to my foxhole where the communications was centered. We spent a while reminiscing until Captain Ashby came over with his last bottle of orange gin. After we killed a better part of the bottle and shot some bull, we headed toward our respective foxholes

Alone, I checked in with my 1st Sergeant for the latest news, and with nothing new coming down, prepared to get some shut-eye. It had been almost 36 hours since I had done any sleeping other than dozing now and then. For some strange reason, I was not a bit sleepy. I sat on the edge of my foxhole, noticing how everything was so still and quiet…a beautiful night. millions of stars in the sky. Made me think back to the days when I was a small boy sitting on the porch of my Grandparents little homestead shack in New Mexico with my Grandmother, listening to crickets chirp and the occasional snort of one of Granddads' horses in the shed out back. Those same stars were shining then just like now. Then the strains of "Silent Night" came drifting across the sky, a haunting harmonica, music being played somewhere by some other soldier…I broke down. Maybe grown men and hardened soldiers aren't supposed to cry, but at that point in time this soldier had tears running down his cheeks, and no regrets. This was my first Christmas away from home.

The next day Captain Ashby took a convoy of trucks into Manila and emptied out the food warehouses. Just for us, it would have been enough to last for the duration, but it was divided equally with the other units. The only things not divided were three cases of "Golden Wedding" and "Canadian Club" whiskey. Chow is chow, but booze was something else and hard to come by. A few days later Capt. Ashby got transferred to Headquarters G-2 and most of the whiskey went with him. He did leave four of us a bottle of Canadian Club each. We held it for a special occasion, and unless someone found it, it is still buried on that ridge where we spent the three months before we surrendered. Maybe some Filipino found it and had a celebration.

We stayed in the Hermosa cane patch until New Years' eve. Then came "March Order " again. This time we only moved across the bridge to a rice paddy, dug foxholes and retired to some rice straw stacks to sleep out the night and await the inevitable raid of the Japanese the next day. Came dawn and also the Jap. They came really early. Time to hit the foxhole. Surprise. The foxhole was half-full of water. Some rice paddies are sub-irrigated and during the night our foxholes had water seeping in. Oh well, we did need a bath.

I shall always remember January 1, 1942, along with December 8, 1941. During the early hours of the afternoon, after about the umpteenth raid to knock out the bridge, our telephone went dead. The Jap bomber must have hit our wires that were strung across the river bottom where the bridge was situated. We did not string the wires across the bridge for fear one of our trucks might get caught up in them. It was the dry season in the Philippines and there was no water in the river, so we ran out wires 50 or 60 yards from the bridge across the river bottom. Both Shelton and Moore were needed on the guns, so that left the Corporal, Yours Truly, to do the job. I shouldered my trusty 1903 Springfield rifle, a test phone, wire cutters and tape and headed out toward the bridge, hoping the Jap would lay off for 30 or 45 minutes.

I had no trouble finding the break. There was a bomb crater that looked to be about where the wires had crossed. Sure enough, I found the break and proceeded to splice it. With trembling hands, one eye peeled on the sky, the other on the repairs, I managed to get the wires spliced and taped up in a reasonable facsimile of the way I had been taught in communication school. I'd just finished plugging in the test phone and checking both ends when the AA guns opened up. Glancing up, I saw dive-bombers heading my way with 500 lb bombs hanging from their bellies. Figuring they had not been hitting their target, I grabbed up my rifle and phone and headed for some boulders this side of the bridge. I barely reached the boulders before I heard a whistle and a bomb hit not 20 feet from where I had been working fifteen seconds before, plunging through a Filipino shack and blowing it into a thousand pieces. Later, we learned the family had taken refuge under the shack. Again, I got the same feeling I had the day they hit Clark Field.

I must have stayed among the boulders for five minutes before venturing out. I knew a lot of bombs had hit and my ears were ringing like mad, but I wasn't sure if there were more to come or not. The first thing that caught my eyes was how many people had gathered around the hole in the ground left by the bomb. That's when I learned of the family's demise. I didn't stay long enough to extend my condolences, but started back to the safety of my wet foxhole only to see that another bomb had knocked the wires out again. Downright disgusting. I did not waste any time making the necessary repairs one more time, going through the same trembling, one eye on the sky, one on the wire procedure I'd used before. I am afraid my communication instructor would have been disappointed in me. This was no time for beauty. The quickest job in this case, was the best. A quick plug-in told me the repairs were O. K. I hadn't gotten the phone unplugged before the ack-ack opened up again. "Not again," I breathed half-aloud, not bothering to unplug the phone as I headed for the boulders again. This time the AA guns got close enough to break up the formation and they scattered the neighborhood with bombs, missing the bridge completely. Coming out from the boulders after being pelted with flying rocks, I returned to the phone and picked up the receiver to see if I was still in business. One bomb looked like it had hit pretty close to the first platoon, but everything was fine. Everything was, in fact, too fine. We were getting orders to move out, but they couldn't get word through to the first, third and fourth platoons. No, not again. Sure enough, the wires were blown out again, 400 yards up the road. Promising to notify the other platoons we were moving out, I headed up the road to the break and hooked on to other end of the break and got through to the other groups, then hightailed it back to my platoon to get my gear and get the hell out of there. I had had my fill of that place. About 5:30 p.m., we were on our way. Shortly thereafter, we heard a loud explosion and were told that all the troops were across the bridge and the engineers had blown it up to keep the Japanese from using it. We had just said goodbye to the outside world. We arrived in rest camp later that night, not bothering to do anything except find a flat spot to lay the body…and get some much-needed sleep.

Rest camp was just what the name implied. It gave us a chance to get our wits together, take a much needed bath, and make sick call for an assortment of maladies brought on from loss of sleep, lack of cleanliness and proper hygiene and going without removing the shoes for days on end. I had a terrible case of athletes' foot. The medic took one look at my feet and told me to go wade in Manila Bay, which was only a couple hundred yards from where we were bivouacked. The rest area was deep into the Bataan peninsula between the two towns of Lamao and Limay. It was deeply wooded, so there was little need for camouflage, since we only went to the beach after dark. The Japanese were flying observation planes daily, so the longer we could remain hidden, the better. There were several units in this same area. All here for the same reason. The three days we were there were so quiet and peaceful, you would not have known there was a war going on. The Japanese had moved into Manila on New Years Day and were throwing a big celebration. Why they would celebrate moving into Manila, an open city from the first week of hostilities, we never knew or particularly gave a damn. We sure were not arguing the point. The rest we were getting due to their frivolities was appreciated.

After the second night of wading in the sea, my feet look like a set of new feet. By the time we pulled out, they were completely well. I can attest to the curative values of this water. Maybe it was the high mineral content. In any case, that Medic sure knew what he was talking about. I had many other occasions after we reached Bataan Field to further check out the benefits of bathing and wading in the sea. We were able to spear some fish to supplement our meager rations while taking the sea water constitutional.

After the evacuation of Clark Field the remaining pursuit aircraft evacuated with us and were operating from small fields thrown up here and there on Bataan. The bombers flew south and were operating from Java and Sumatra. With the completion of Bataan field on the Manila Bay coast between Limay and Cabcaban the pursuits were being based there. It was to be a permanent field sufficiently large enough to handle bombers should the occasion arise.

On January 4, 1942, after the third day in rest camp, we received orders to move out. Bataan Field was our destination and protection of Bataan Field our objective. Our platoon position was some 500 yards off the west end of the field on top of a ridge that ran sort of parallel to the field on down to the Bay. We manned this position for the next three months, until we were surrendered.

We moved in during the night, set up camp and were ready to break up a dogfight early the next morning between two P-40s who were just taking off, heavily loaded to strafe and bomb Japanese front line positions, and a Jap Zero. Because the P-40s were so low and loaded, the Zero had somewhat of an edge. The P-40 was not built for low level maneuvering so the Zeros could run rings around them at low altitudes. After a few rounds from our 50-caliber machine guns (an air-cooled 50 taken off one of the destroyed B-17s and mounted on a makeshift tripod, held down by four sacks of cement) and the 37s changed the Zeros' mind. He headed for a safer place. The P-40s, far as I know, competed their mission and returned to their base.

The rest of January saw spasmodic raids on Bataan fields, doing very little damage the air corps engineers couldn't repair within minutes after each raid. Things around our position, generally, were quiet...so quiet, rumors started that we were going to be moved up to the front lines to give AA fire, thus keeping the Jap off our field artillery batteries. Some of the 37 mm-platoons did eventually go to the front lines, doing just that, but we never received such an assignment.

I Was There, Charley

Shortly after we took up our position at Bataan field, Captain Ashby (he had received a field promotion) was transferred to the 515th CAC Headquarters as G-2 and Reconnaissance. This really knocked a hole in the morale of our platoon, as Capt. Ashby had been father, brother, buddy and leader to all of us. Our loss wasn't soon forgotten. We believed anyone sent to replace him would just be a figurehead. We operated without an officer in charge until Sgt. Luther Ragsdale from Pinon, New Mexico was sent in as acting platoon leader. Even after an officer was assigned to our platoon, Sgt Ragsdale ran it.

After the first three weeks at Bataan field, we felt that we were no longer a part of the war, as there was a lull in fighting everywhere. We saw an observation type plane about twice a day. There were several rumors to explain the Japanese inactivity. Some had it they were stricken with cholera and malaria fever, others that our forces on the front line were stronger than the Japanese anticipated and they were waiting for reinforcements. The latter seemed to be right, because about the middle of March they started in, and until the time of our surrender, their field artillery pounded the front lines night and day. Behind the lines, we got worked over trying to keep the dive-bombers off Bataan field. We were on alert 24 hours a day, the last two weeks not getting any sleep at all. We were so keyed-up, we probably wouldn't have slept if we could have. With rations reduced to 1/8th, the handwriting on the wall was getting easier to read

By the end of February, thousands of Filipino refugees were streaming into Bataan, fleeing the over 500,000 Japanese soldiers crowding the island. The food situation became critical. We were on half rations by then, and the extra refugee mouths to feed did not help the situation any. We went from half rations to quarter rations and by the time we surrendered, we were on a starvation ration of one-eighth, which consisted of rice, canned salmon or horsemeat and powdered milk. Once, sometimes twice, bread was baked in a makeshift bakery at Marvales and issued to us. The men on front lines were eating C-rations when they could get them. The Japanese didn't beat us, lack of food did it for them.

Those of us behind the lines were a little more fortunate than those on the front lines. When the chow started being cut, we could do a little scavenging. Filipino banana patches were not safe for several kilometers around. We even learned the eatable roots, fruits and wild animals. Monkeys, wild chickens, wild pigs, mouse deer, iguana lizards - they all became belly fillers. Even Cavalry horses were turned into fare for the day. The carabao, or malay water buffalo, the 'beast of burden' in the Philippines, were tied by their owners' side to keep them from becoming a G. I. meal. A hungry stomach has no conscience.

Casualties ran into the hundreds and even thousands. Bodies were buried from one end of the island to the other, most of them near where they had fallen. The more fortunate bodies were buried in hastily dug graves in a schoolyard near Marvales. This place became an interment for those who lost their lives fighting, and rightly so. Marvales had been completely destroyed in the early days of the conflict and the burned ruins served as a stark grave marker for the cemetery. Most of the men, including me, unpatriotic as it may sound to those who were not there, were fighting to keep alive another day. We felt we had been drug into a fight that was uncalled for, and now it was us or them. It wasn't the rights of the Filipinos, or any other patriotic gesture that kept us going. It was self- preservation. We could not have called ourselves professional soldiers, as there wasn't one among us who wouldn't have given up ten years of pay just to be back in the good old U.S.A. Or any safe place, for that matter. We would have fought as long as there was a breath in our bodies, but it was a case of the coyote with his back to the wall, fighting for his life. We'd run as far as we could run.

Out of sentiment for the men who now lie at Marvales came this ironic bit of philosophy. I don't know who wrote it, but with all due respect to him, I am including it in this book. It was good enough to be published by the Japanese after we were taken prisoners, in one of the Manila papers.

THE LEVELER

Death is a great leveler they say.
But in Marvales' Gods Acre
There is a mausoleum that stands against
morality and is proud.
There is a rain worn, wind washed cross and
sun baked.
A pitiable gesture against obliteration.
And yonder is grass, the undistinguishable trace
of mould and more grass.
Yet in the Military interment area Km 178
Rows and rows of plots,
Bamboo crosses receding in column formation.
No General, no soldier here.
In this severely simple beauty of likeness akin to pain,
Only plots and crosses and comrades.
Death is a great leveler, they say.
(Author unknown)

The Japanese made several attempts to establish a beachhead behind our lines, both on the Manila Bay side and the Chine Sea side. The bloodiest attempt came at Agaloma Bay. A well coordinated attack by the Jap with excellent cover from the air and sea. In fact, some 400 Japanese managed to get on land only to be hunted down like animals. It was bloody, and I am talking about the Japanese losses. The better part of the 14th Division, veterans of the sacking and raping of China, Indo-China and the Malay straits were wiped out. We shifted everything from hand guns to field artillery, including some 37 mm AA guns to that side of the peninsula to ward off the attack. It was during this siege that the clipped wing Air Corps personnel turned in a royal job fighting as infantrymen.

Probably the best job by any air corps group was the endless missions flown by the few remaining P-40s, loading up bombs, taking off, dumping their loads and strafing, then returning to their respective bases and repeating that routine 24 hours a day during the three-day attack. Barge load after barge load of Japanese troops were sunk by these repeated forays. One of our men, a truck driver of a halftrack with a mounted 75 mm field gun of the 88th field artillery said it was like stomping baby duck in the mud. But you sunk one barge and there was another to take its place.

The real fighting came in the final cleanup of the few Japanese that managed to make the beach. It was mass slaughter for Jap, but their snipers holed up in the rocky clefts of Agaloma Bay took their toll of the U.S.-Filipino troops. Two gunboats were sent in to blast them out because they wouldn't surrender. One or two were captured but wouldn't talk and soon died of the wounds they had received. This was the first U.S.-Filipino troop experience with the suicidal mania of the Nips.

On the Manila side of the peninsula several attempts were made to establish a beach head behind the lines Most of them were thought to be merely feelers and were broken up either by 37 mm AA guns leveled to make like field artillery or 8" inch rifle fire from Corriegdor. Tanks and half-tracks with 75 mm field guns mounted on them were also used in these attacks. Constant patrols were made along the cost line from Balanga on the east side to Bigac on the west. The rugged coastline of Bataan was in our favor in the Japanese attempts to establish a beach head.

The big drive started about the first of April. Behind the lines, we knew what was up. The Japanese heretofore had used only light dive-bombers in their attacks on the front line and behind-the-line installations, but now they started using everything they had. There was a constant stream of bombers, both big and light, bombing the fronts lines, Bataan and Cabcaban air fields and now Corriegdor. Until this time, Corriegdor had been getting little or no bombing, but now the Japanese were hitting Corriegdor to quiet the big coast artillery guns that were menacing their drive into Bataan. The ack-ack guns on Corriegdor took their toll of Japanese planes dropping their bombs on the tiny fortified island.

Day and night Anti-craft guns and field artillery could be heard barking out their defiance of the advancing Japanese troops. The massive flood of Japanese troops was too much for the half-starved and weary troops at the front. First the Filipino Army troops who had had very little training prior to the Japanese invasion and had received the brunt of the enemy constant pounding for the past three months, starved and sick with Malaria and dysentery, lost their fight. Completely giving up, they started pouring in from the front line like bees from a hive. This left the few Americans in the 31st Infantry Regiment, the few Americans and Filipino Scouts in the field artillery, the 194th and 192nd tank battalions and the clipped wing air corps infantry holding the lines. Out-numbered 100 to 1, they too had to fall back. We watched, from our gun position high on a ridge overlooking the highway, the steady flow of troop in retreat. As we watched we knew before long we would be front line and next to withdraw.

After spending the day of April 8,1941 in suspense, watching the constant un-ending steam of tired and weary troops straggling below our gun position, we began to get nervous. Late in the afternoon, after hours of bombing, we decided to call battery headquarter and see what was going down. Instead, headquarters got through to us with orders to destroy guns and equipment and fall back to Kilometer 162 near Cabcaban Airfield.

By this time, so many trucks had been wrecked or worn out, or commandeered by other units, we only had one truck that would run. Disabling all equipment and guns, we packed our barracks bags and, with the first platoon in a two and one half ton truck made our way toward Km. 162.

It was after dark before the battery was again assembled, at which time we were notified that we no longer were an ack-ack outfit, but infantry, and to govern ourselves as such. About an hour later our Battery Commander called us all together and told us that outside of a few tanks and half-tracks, we were the only thing between where we were and the Jap. In short, we were the front line.

The front line had been set up as the ridge running along the edge of Cabcaban field. Each battery was assigned a position on this ridge. The ridge ran from the bay back to the Marveles Mountains, a distance of 10 miles or more and we had some 1500 men to man it.

For the third time since December 8, 1941, I got a certain feeling in the pit of my stomach. Not so much that I was afraid...it was more a feeling of apprehension - of not knowing what was going to happen. We had so little knowledge of infantry tactics, plus the fact our only weapons were our rifles and bayonets with, at the most, 200 rounds of ammunition. This against an onslaught of tanks, artillery, mortars, bombers and just about any weapon at their command. With this array of fighting implements, we had about as much chance as a snowball in hell, to use a very apt, trite expression.

We spent the dragging hours of that night amidst the rumble of the big 12 inch rifles on Corriegdor, firing round after round over our heads into the advancing Japs to the north of us. As if that was not hell enough, Mother Nature turned loose with a series of tremors that shook us to our feet as we stumbled in the darkness, through brush and thorn thickets to find our position on the ridge.

Along about 3 a.m. on the morning of April 9 1941, through shouts and cat-calls (if there had been any Jap around we would have been dead ducks), while still looking for a position, our battery commander reported in that he had found it. So back through the same thickets and underbrush we went, and by 5 a.m., located ourselves and were digging in for the inevitable last stand. Thirsty, hungry, tired to the bone, downhearted, and lost. From where we were appraising the situation, it looked like another Custer massacre, this time at the hands of the little, slant-eyed Nippon warriors instead of the Indians. By now we had committed ourselves to extinction, or so we thought. It was rumored from the beginning the Nips did not take prisoners, so we had two options: stay and fight or risk desertion charges and take to the hills; somehow, the hills just did not look as tempting as you might think. Maybe we were soldiers after all, fighting for what we believed in. In any case, we stayed. We all stayed. ALL OF US. Glued to our rifles awaiting the unknown.

Through the remainder of the dark hours, we silently watched as dawn turned the surrounding woods into shadows of light and dark Little by little we could make out objects on the airfield below, but nothing that looked like the enemy had arrived. Then, as the sun poked its head over the horizon, we heard the roar of aircraft as several Zeros came down the ridge spreading shrapnel bombs, then returned, strafing madly up and down until they expended their gun belts. Needless to say, we had no option other than to cringe in the depth of our respective foxholes we had just spent the last two hours digging. After 30 to 45 minutes, it was over. At the rate they were going, we would never live to see any hand-to-hand combat, because these continued air forays sooner or later would take care of us all. We'd either be dead or so disoriented we would be unable to put up a fight. It was while laying low in my foxhole I thought about Joyce Kilmer's poem, 'Trees' that I had memorized way back in the fifth grade and which inspired me to write a parody I called "Foxholes." I have included it below:

FOXHOLES

I think when the bomb-raid sirens toll,
There is nothing as nice as a deep foxhole.
A hole in which you can sit and pray,
    for safety to pray another day.

A hole that is six feet, three and deep,
That can, at night, be used for sleep.

One where you may sit and wait
The lead of a straefer's tete-a-tete.

Into whose depth you're bound to drop,
When mortar shells begin to pop.

God made the world and things untold,
But he just didn't make enough foxholes.

    During this episode word came down through that chow was being served down the line a ways. In spite the raids, we left positions and everything, creeping on all-fours to make our way to a bamboo thicket where we found our chow truck parked and dishing out steaming rice, cooked up with milk, sugar and raisins. To us, it was a real delicacy, especially after eating rice and horsemeat for the past month and half.

While we were gorging ourselves back in our foxholes on the ridge, we received the first dubious but wistful rumor of a surrender. To add to this possibility, we had not seen nor heard the bombers in over an hour. It was as quite as a Sunday morning back in good ole USA. Then, on the other hand, it could be the lull before the grand finale. By 10 a.m., with still no action of any sort, the certainty of a surrender sure seemed in the making.

At 10:30 it was official. We were to start waving white flags up and down the line. White shirts, shorts, underwear, handkerchiefs and anything white came out and was tied to a stick. It was more of a letdown than a relief. A pleasant letdown, strange as that may sound, but I think most of us were just glad it was over. At least glad the suspense was over. There was no sadness as far as I could denote by the actions of the men. No tears of defeat, no moaning over the loss, only an air of speculation. How would we be treated? Surely, with an overall surrender there would be no wholesale slaughter. Where were they? Where would they take us? How? All these questions were going over and over in our minds. We had heard so much of their atrocities in China and elsewhere…would it be any different here? I tried not to think about it. None of us had much to say. It was a very quite bunch of G.I.s who awaited the coming of the Jap. Anyway, these were moments of reflection as we assembled and marched up to a little schoolhouse on a hill overlooking Cabcaban Air Field to lay down our arms.

The majority of the men surrendering that afternoon were members of either the 200th or 515th CACs There were a few stragglers from other American units, but as the front line had been made up of those two regiments, they were the first to surrender. Of course there was no way of checking up then, but about 80 percent of the men of the 200th and the 515th CAC laid down their arms that afternoon. As General King, Commander of the Bataan forces who had arranged for the surrender said later on, "You didn't surrender, I surrendered you." Some members of our units made it to Corriegdor, to surrender 30 days later.

Because we were on the front line and among the first ones to surrender, we were fortunate in that we did not have to walk

I Was There, Charley

the whole distance like so many of those surrendering later on. The Japanese wasted no time in hauling in field artillery to shell Corriegdor, knowing that Corriegdor would not fire back as long as they were holding prisoners in that vicinity, but they did not reckon on an American gunboat anchored of the coast of Corriegdor. Hardly had they started firing until the gunboat matched them round for round. It must have been our lucky day, because the first round from the gunboat was a dud. It hit not twenty feet from where we were grouped, and being the high explosive type, would have killed us and I would not be typing this account today. The two following hit further down the hill, shaking up things in general. The concussion deafened me and left my ears ringing for months afterward. Then one Japanese gun crew was blown to pieces and all us prisoners took off in mass exodus, seeking refugee any place we could find it…most of us hot-footing it down toward the bay and on down the beach to the little barrio, Cabcaban. Here we gathered and were placed under machine gun guard. This did not look good at the time, but later turned out to be only a precautionary measure. During this scramble, a Japanese soldier who was guarding us on the hill, took a swing at me with his rifle butt. It landed just above the right hipbone, knocking me down. I rolled for several feet, hesitating to get up for fear of maybe getting bayoneted. I looked around and saw the Jap dragging ass out of there. He was as scared as the rest of us. I was able to painfully make my way to where the others had stopped, and joined my group.

A little later in the afternoon, another convoy of trucks and soldiers pulling more field artillery arrived and started setting up above us in a grove of trees. As the truck emptied cargo of men, ammunition and equipment, they loaded us prisoners on the trucks like sardines, and headed back up the road to haul in more guns.

The going was slow. Convoy after convoy of field artillery was pouring in to the Bataan peninsula for the siege of Corriedor. Each time we met a convoy, our trucks had to pull off to the side to let them pass. It was here we suffered their harassment. At the snails pace they were moving, the Jap soldiers had plenty of time to hop off their trucks and throw rocks at us, flail us with their rifle rods and even get in the truck and demand we empty our pockets. They took what they wanted or else, the else being anything their depraved minds could think up. Many of the men on the truck I was riding on suffered bruises and cuts from our tormentors. One officer on our truck received broken ribs when he was booted for not handing over a half-pack of Camel cigarettes he had in his shirt pocket.

We passed the last of the convoys around 9 or 10 that night. It seemed like an eternity. An eternity filled with brutality, murder, sadism and hate. An eternity in which we saw and older Filipino woman deliberately rundown by an errant truck driver and left in the road to be run over by other trucks following in its wake. The Filipinos who had followed the army into Bataan, hearing of the surrender, already downhearted, defeated, starved and lost, started the long trek back to their homes carrying their sole belongings on their back. The road on both sides was a continuous stream of homeless humanity caught up in a war not of their making. It was slaughter if one ventured to near the highway. One Filipino was shot down in cold blood for his inability to understand what the Jap wanted him to do. It was blood chilling to watch such inhumanity to humanity. We dared not make a move to look like we disapproved or we would have received the same treatment.

We rode until about 2 a.m. before we were given a rest and a chance to stretch after the past eight hours. They stopped at a small Barrio and dumped us off in what appeared to be some Filipinos chicken pen they had commandeered for the night. It had netting wire around it and smelled strongly of chicken manure. The ground smelled of sewerage. We were allowed to get some semblance of rest and fill our canteens from a pump in one corner of the pen. We'd had very little sleep in the past 60 hours, so in spite of the accommodations, we slept the sleep of the dead.

About 5 a.m. we were awakened, lined up on the edge of the road and started walking. Any hope we would get anything to eat vanished. The road, having been used for the past four months by heavy truck traffic, was churned up into a two to three inch layer of dust, which made walking difficult. The steady trample of the many feet stirred the dust into a cloud that we had to breathe constantly. It looked like we'd jumped out of the frying pan into the fire.

By 7 a.m. the sun was well up and on its earth-scorching trek across the zenith, as only the sun can scorch during the dry season in the tropics. It did not take long for a canteen of water to go in this heat and dust. As the day heated up more and more and with less and less water, it didn't take long for our mouths and throat to became so dry we couldn't spit.

To make matters worse, the truck traffic picked up to the point we had to string out single file. Each convoy that passed stirred up that much more dust until we were all covered with a thin coat of light brown dust. I was not sure where we were or how far we had gone, but one thing I was sure of…we were on the road into Bataan, on the way out. Where it would end was anyone's guess.

Several small barrios were passed with curious Filipinos stealing looks at us and occasionally giving the old V for victory sign. The Japanese guards were in much the same shape as we were and looked just about as bad. By midmorning, a new group of guards took over and we didn't even slow down. When the sun was at it highest, we were ordered to stop and move off the road into a field and sit down. We watched as they proceeded to open their lunch buckets and eat in the shade of some trees while we basked in the sun.

After their leisurely lunch, they ordered us up and away.. Many of the men were beginning to feel the effects of the heat and dust plus no water, and started stumbling along, assisted by fellow prisoners who were in just as bad shape. The Jap guards would yell and prod us with the ends of their rifles. It looked like they were seeing how far they could drive us without out food or water. I could have gone a long way without food, but lack of water brings on dehydration and then, that is all she wrote. We had to get water soon or there would be no tomorrow. Maybe that is what they wanted.

Late in the afternoon, we arrived at a small Barrio and they changed guards again. We thought we might get water here but they were only changing guards. As soon as the new guards took over, we were on our way again. Joy of joys, we only walked a short distance to an open field where we were directed to sit down in a sort of circle while they took up station just outside the circle. After awhile, four carts, pulled by carabao, carrying large drums, approached the area. The guards situated them in four different areas around the circle and directed five or six of us at a time, to come to a cart. The barrels were filled with water. We did not question the quality but as fast as we could, filled our canteens and moved on so others could do the same. After everyone had made his trip to the cart, the guards motioned that there was still water and come and get it. I think most of us were able to refill our canteens before the guards had the cart driver to move on.

What next? That was the question. The guards gradually gathered into groups of two or three, seeming to relax their vigilance as they obviously were engaging in a bull session. When it appeared that was it for the night, we began to look for a place to flake out. The water had helped tremendously and somewhat revived our bodies as well as our spirits. I lay back, using the old steel helmet for a pillow, only to be awakened sometime later by the noise of the guards being changed. In the dark, I could make out POWs sitting up, although most seemed to be sleeping or resting their eyes. I lay awake for some time, reliving the past day and its deprivation. Was this an indication of what we were to expect for the future? Could it get any worse? Hunger pangs were getting worse and worse. We'd gone more than 48 hours without food, under the most grueling circumstances. I must have fallen asleep. I was suddenly jolted awake by loud shouting – it was the Japanese prodding us to get on the way.

Being unfamiliar with the country, I had no idea where we were. Lined up, I was beside an older soldier who said he was in the 31st infantry and had been in the Philippines for several years. When the subject came up about location, he thought we were not too far from San Fernando. The trucks had taken us further than I thought, because I though we were still in Bataan. We were not making very good time in spite of the constant harassing of the Jap guards. By midmorning, there was another guard change and at noon, another stop while they ate lunch. One Guard, a bit more talkative than most, told the men at the head of the column that we would be in San Fernando soon for a takusan (big) celebration. Our imaginations went wild at that announcement.

By the time we reached San Fernando, we were completely dehydrated again. There were rumors of food and water there, although food was the farthest thing from our minds because we needed water. Even a drop to moisten our cracking lips would have helped. As it turned out, there was a celebration, but it was at our expense. We were lined up, four abreast and, as the Jap guard counted in Japanese, we marched down the street in front of what appeared to be the Japanese Headquarters. Filipinos lined both sides of the streets. It was quite a show for them, determined as they were to impress the Filipinos of their own superiority, thereby further degrading us the only way they knew how: humiliation.

Afterward, a few blocks from the celebration, we were directed into a warehouse district and crowded into a large open pen, told to sit and wait in the sun. This seemed like a small favor, as it was getting late in the afternoon and getting a little cooler, or maybe just less hot. Just before dark, some more carts came in with water and, finally, food. The Guards used three of the stronger appearing men to dish up the rice. There was plenty to go around, but horror of horrors, it had set in the sun since being cooked and had gone sour. You don't look a gift horse in the mouth, so, hungry as we were, we ate it. We would have eaten it if maggots were crawling in it. I ate some and saved some, not knowing what the morrow would bring.

We spent the night there and were awakened the next morning to face a new bunch of guards. Again, we were lined up and shook down. The picking was light and those guards, disappointed at not finding anything worthwhile, started roughing up the men because they didn't have anything. By now, all I had was the dust-covered sweaty clothes I had on, the shoes and socks that had not been off my feet in 72 hours, my canteen, mess kit, billfold with five, 1-peso bills in it and three tins of c-ration powdered coffee. I had forgotten, until later on, that one of the tins had a 17-jewel wristwatch sans band, and my Texas Tech Class Ring. Much later at Cabanatuan,

I traded the watch for some quinine. I still have my class ring. The Jap are tea-sippers and coffee did not appeal to the guard that roughly searched me. He took the 5 pesos, elbowed me in the middle and moved on. Some of those guards were just naturally mean and brutal. I heard of the West Point officer that could not get his ring off…they cut his finger off to get to that ring.

Shortly after leaving San Fernando, we stopped for a convoy coming out of Lingayan Gulf. Here, I had the misfortune of watching one of the most brutal and sadistic acts one human can impose on another. Several Filipinos were filing across a rice paddy on the embankment that separated one paddy from another, Indian fashion one after the other, to cross the highway to get into town. All of them made it across the highway, except a young couple. The mother, obviously pregnant and carrying a small baby in her arms, was trailing behind a short distance. The Jap advance guard stopped them and would not let them cross until the convoy had passed. From our short distance, it was evident there was some sort of confrontation. We could hear their voices, but not being learned in the Japanese or Tagalog language, we could not know what it was about. The Jap was patting down the male and came up with something the Filipino was reluctant to give up. When the male reached toward the soldier, the Jap stepped back, raised his rifle and bayoneted the Filipino in the gut. Our ears were immediately filled with the screams of the wife as she dropped the baby to the ground and fell prostrate across her husband's body. The Jap guard casually raised his rifle and drove the bayonet between the woman's shoulder blades, then, withdrawing the blade calmly, he casually pocketed something and joined his comrades at the rear of the convoy.

We were too stunned to do anything…afraid any motion would bring the guard's wrath down on us. We stood dumfounded, hardly wanting to believe what we had just seen. It was like a bad dream. It must have been a bad dream. I still have them. Yet, there they were, the two bodies thrashing in the last throes of death, pouring forth their life blood from wounds so brutally and heartlessly administered, with a small helpless baby crying in the blood of its own mother and father. Why hadn't the guard killed the child? A question we will never have answered. There was a great deal of speculation later as we plodded on to the railroad siding where we were packed like sardines in a little old box car with no ventilation for the next two or three hours on a ride to Capas, our last stop before a long 10 mile hike to Camp O,Donnell, our destination.

I thought we had had it rough already, but nothing compared to that ride in that sardine can. Most of the men were already suffering from Malaria and after eating the sour rice, some of them developed a diarrhea. This is something over which you have no control. Packed as tight as we were no one had to draw a picture of the conditions by the time we detrained at Capas. There was no excuse for the overcrowding. There were at least 25 empty boxcars on that siding and they packed 500 men in four cars with one engine pulling them. The Japanese set out to systematically exterminate us in the most humiliating, degrading and suffering manner, which was confirmed in a speech from the commandant of the prison camp when we arrived. The ten-mile walk from the railhead in the blazing sun further weakened the already sick prisoners. We were just running on will power, adrenaline and pride.

Clemens A. Kathman

CHAPTER THREE
O'DONNELL, HELL-HOLE OF CREATION
APRIL 12, 1942--JUNE 1, 1942

O'Donnell, a name that will forever remain in my mind as synonymous with dirt, filth, sickness, disease, cruelty, brutality, depravity…you name it. The Japs used every insidious way their depraved minds could think of to reduce the POWs to the lowest form of crawling, mewling creatures.

This camp had been and old Philippine Army training camp, and was thrown up quickly when the government realized the inevitability of war in their homeland. It was some two Kilometers from the town of O'Donnell and 100 kilometers north of Manila, on the highway to Lingayan Gulf. Due to the haste in which the camp was built, it was little better than stalls for animals. The barracks were constructed of bamboo strips and covered by rice straw. Into each barrack, possibly 30 feet long and 15 feet wide, 100 men were crammed. These barracks were constructed so that there were two tiers, one above the other, with bamboo slats to lie on. Imagine a sick and diseased man with dysentery bunking above you. Not pleasant. At best, it was waterproof, thanks to the jack-of-all-uses 'rice straw.' It was dry season anyway, and most of us just bunked on the ground.

As soon as we arrived, we were again shaken down and gone over with a fine-toothed comb. Then a short, skinny, syphilitic Jap looking like something out of a comic book, a Major, climbed upon a box to get himself above us so he could harangue us for the next 30 minutes. He wore the finely polished black boots that was the definite mark of a Japanese officer. His pants, with baggy bottoms, were tucked sloppily into the tops of his boots. His shirt resembled a summer sport shirt, with its air vents under the arms, white and red felt-looking epaulets on the shoulders with gold stripes and stars pined on the tip of each collar. Wearing the usual tropic helmet, he was a good caricature of a clown. With my apologies to the clowns. As he swaggered back and forth on the box, spewing his venom, his left hand constantly pushing forward the hilt of the long sword that was suspended from the belt around his waist, to keep it from dragging on the top of the box. As I gazed at this monstrosity with the black gay nineties mustache and beady eyes, I wondered where the anthropologist had been all these years in their search for the "missing link."

Nevertheless, after spouting off for about thirty minutes, he turned to a pimpish-looking collaborationist that formerly had worked in the PX at Clark Field as a general flunky boy to interpret what he had just said. The Filipino, if that was what he was, interpreter stretched himself to the height of his importance and proceeded to give his interpretation of "Beetle-Brows" diatribe.

"I am Major so-in-so of the Japanese Imperial Army," he stated. "You are my enemies. You are enemies of the Japanese Imperial Government and you will be treated as such. You cannot expect any leniency whatsoever. You have surrendered to our might and must suffer the consequences. You will obey all our orders given you by us. You will be given food and shelter, but in turn you must work for it. As long as you obey all orders that are given, you will be treated fairly. Any infraction of the rules means the death sentence. We did not ask that you surrender. The Japanese soldiers do not surrender, but fight to the death for the Emperor and country before being taken. This is the honorable way. Do not expect any sympathy, but make the best of your misfortune." There was a lot of other bull but mostly reiteration of what he had already said.

When the interpreter finished his dire warnings, he appointed an American officer to take charge of the in-camp operations and guards assigned men to their rats nest, called barracks. Too tired to fix the rice floor sweepings and rotten sweet potatoes, most men flaked out, sleeping the sleep of the dead.

From then on for the next three weeks it was a continuous sweat from day to day watching and waiting for the remainder of our various units to arrive. They were arriving tired, haggard, footsore, starved and half dead from disease and mistreatment on the infamous "Death March." There were those who toughed it out only to die a few days later. Some so dead on their feet, they were out for days. Still others, who fared better, refreshed after a good days rest, related the horrible ordeal they had endured.

Some walked continuously for as long as ten days, covering a distance of 200 kilometers without food and what little water they could filch or was given along the way. Often the water they managed to sneak was at the risk of being shot, or was obtained from streams polluted by carcasses of bodies, those killed in the last big push, along with dung from the animals that sought water in the dry season. This they drank as a last resort, exposing themselves to the many diseases and worms that the tropics are known for. Sleeping in the open fields or in some carabao wallow they had been herded into, fighting mosquitoes and other type insects, is it any wonder they had malaria and dysentery.

These men told of unnumbered incidents of beatings because they lingered along the way, too tired to keep up. Sometimes they were bayoneted, constantly kept on the move. They told of seeing friendly Filipinos being beaten for offering them aid or giving the V for victory sign. Walk, walk, walk…one foot in front of the other one more step nearer, to what? The Jap guards changed every few miles, still the POWs walked on. Many fell by the wayside, too fatigued to go on. These men were shot, bayoneted or when lucky, got picked up by a truck and carried to the next stop. All this at the whim of whichever Jap was on guard at the time. Some of the more desperate men managed to creep off into the bush at night to be picked up by friendly natives and smuggled into the hills to join the guerilla bands that were already organizing. A few went crazy and took their own lives. Such were the unbelievable tales of horror that came in with each bunch.

The Jap guards told them that as soon as they got to San Fernando they could ride the rest of the way. What the Jap failed to tell them was the condition under which they would make this trip. They, like us, were packed in those little boxcars, 100 or more with just one opening where the Jap guard stood, almost covering the only source of fresh air. We thought we had it bad when we were forced to make this ride, but these men had it worse. And as a result, they were a lot weaker, sicker, and more despondent from the many days on the road. They passed out like we did. but a lot more of them passed out. If a man passed out or died there was no room for him to fall. He remained in his position just like one sardine in a can of sardines. One tale told of a Colonel, crazed by the heat and the past torturous days, flung himself and a Jap guard out of the car and off a bridge into the water below.

By the end of the third week, most of the men who hadn't died along the way arrived in the camp. All had gotten the same welcoming speech from the clown major at the gate. A few men straggled in later. A check-up was made of our battery and only two or three men were unaccounted for, but other batteries were not so fortunate. At least we were all together again and as uncertain as it seemed, we would face it, hopefully, together.

The first consideration upon our arrival was chow. We had gone so long on short rations before the surrender and, having very little to eat on the way out of Bataan, we had hopes the situation would be better here, but it did not look like it. The kitchens were in a state of disarray, having been torn up when the Filipinos evacuated the post. Water for kitchen use had to be carried from a small river a short distance from the camp. This was done by groups of two men with a pole on their shoulders, from which was suspended a half of a 55 gallon drum filled with water. As the river was polluted with all sorts of filth, this water had to be boiled before it could be used, either for cooking or for drinking purposes. This situation remained for two or three weeks before workers could repair the filtration plant.

To start with, after the speech we received at the gate, we were expecting the bare necessities for existence. The drawback was not the quantity of the food, but the quality. The rice resembled floor sweepings and the vegetables issued were wilted or rotting. Many of the cooks had no experience cooking rice. Instead of steaming it, they boiled it to a thick gruel like mess called "lugao." For those already suffering from diarrhea and dysentery, this only aggravated the condition. Vegetables boiled without any seasoning left little to be desired from men already too weaken and without appetite.

Most of the sick men went through chow line, got their ration, only to walk to the nearest latrine and dump it. Or maybe, after persistent nagging on the part of a buddy urging him to eat or he would die, he'd try to eat, only to vomit it up a few minutes later. Others didn't bother to go through the food line, leaving the cooks in a quandary of what to do with pots of rice and vegetables. They knew if they threw it away the Jap would see it and cut rations severely. The overflow was thrown in the latrines and sanitation crews would cover the old latrines and dig new ones the next day, hoping the Jap didn't make any surprise inspections.

The mess halls or kitchens were built similar to the barracks, with a furnace-like structure of concrete in one end. The furnace was nothing more than a large concrete box-like affair probably 10 ft long, three feet wide and three feet in depth. Into the top three holes two and a half feet in diameter, rested the large "kawas" (a cast iron pot resembling the old wash pots used by the early settlers for rendering lard, making soap and a hundred and one other uses). The "Kawa" was not as deep as the wash pot but bigger in circumference. In one end of this firebox was a chimney and on the side under each pot was an opening for inserting fuel.

To cook, "Kawas" were placed in the holes, water added, and fires built in the firebox heating the water as the flames passed under the pots and out the chimney. In this manner, rice could be cooked by placing a large wooden top over the pot, keeping the steam in. Vegetables could be either steamed or boiled in the same manner.

Cooking for four or five hundred men at one time proved to be an undertaking in itself. It was a simple matter to put rice and vegetable in water and let them boil or steam until they were well done. But using just three Kawas made it impossible to cook enough for that many men at one time without emptying and cooking another batch. This was the problem that confronted the cooks and K.P.s. when they took over the kitchen. The Jap did very little to alleviate the situation. Several 55-gallon steel drums were brought in but they were rusted and smelled of gasoline. It took backbreaking and endless work to scrub them until they were usable.

There were piles of scrap lumber in the vicinity of our camp. Securing hammers, saws and nails and permission from the Jap, the cooks were able to construct large troughs to empty the rice and veggies into. These did smell of rosin and wood, but was a far cry from the gagging odor of gasoline that permeated the food and caused an already finicky stomach to turn over. As the wooden troughs were used and scrubbed over and over, the odor diminished to the point of hardly being noticeable.

Many men, like me, were caught short when we were captured. On the night before Bataan fell and we were ordered to fall back to Cabcaban field, my sole belongings were tied in a bunk roll and barracks bag. The barracks bag was discarded along he way. All that remained was my bedroll, rifle, bayonet, 200 round of ammunition, canteen, canteen cup, mess kit, spoon, clothes on my back, shoes on my feet and a steel helmet. After surrendering, the load was lightened by turning in the rifle, bayonet and ammunition.

I never knew a steel helmet had so many uses until then. It had been a burdensome load we were ordered to carry with us at all times. On the night we formed the front line, we were ordered to wear those helmets. Most of us wore them for the psychological peace of mind more than for the protection they gave us. These 1918 models were very little protection, but later I was glad I had mine with me. It turned out to be mess kit, washbasin, pillow, laundry tub, chair and any one of a dozen other uses.

Hollow bamboo tubes were split in half and used for mess kits for those not lucky enough to get into camp with their mess kits. Many tin cans became cups or food containers for some POWs. Numerous times I've seen a man coming from the chow line with his rice dumped on the flat surface of a plank picked up out of the scrap heap, his vegetables in his canteen cup and, if he was lucky, a corned-beef can of some other make shift implement for a spoon or fork.

Imagine our joy if we were able to get possession of a can of stateside food. A lot of this did get into the camp, smuggled and first and later admitted by the Jap. Men working on outside details such as rice hauling, wood chopping and telephone line repair details were often taken to some small barrio and allowed to purchase available items if they had cash on hand. After the natives got wise that there was some money still available, they were allowed to hawk their wares at the work place or on the way to and from work. Prices for the articles were ten times their original. Then, after being brought into camp and resold to those not so fortunate to work outside, the price doubled or tripled again. Corned beef sold for $5 a can. A nickel Hershey bar sold for a dollar or more. A small can of cocoa brought $8 to $10. These are just a few examples of black marketing that went on.

In spite of this situation existing and food being sold at these outrageous prices, it was small in comparison to the lives that it helped to save. Many men, unable to eat the steamed rice and vegetables, did manage to keep a little of this canned "gold" down and it probably saved their lives. The only drawback here was that there were too few men who could afford the price of this life saving black marketing. Many died, longing for a taste of real chow, watching as a bunkmate gorged himself with corned beef, sardines, Spam, Vienna Sausages or some other canned product. It was a survival of the fittest in the raw. There was no place for sentiment or brotherly love. It was either you or me. I got mine, you see if you can get yours. As I said, a hungry stomach has no conscience.

Second only to the food situation in the death rate was sanitation. Not that O'Donnell was dirtier than any other place on the island, but when you concentrate that many men in a place that small, with no previous plans for incarceration, there had to be sanitation problems. If half of these persons are sick and disabled, the problem is magnified. It takes time to work out these situations and it was unfortunate that these were not the best of times to do that. Consequently many lives were lost. I was there over two months before moving to Cabanatuan. Some progress had been made by then, but they were still a long way from acceptable.

From the moment we first entered the camp, a safe water source was the number one problem. A lack of clean water for drinking, cooking, washing dishes, food containers, clothes and for bathing and medicinal purposes contributed more to the death rate and any other factor. Food containers stank of soured food from lack of enough water to adequately wash and rinse them. Mess kits or other makeshift eating utensils were given a lick and a promise to do better next time if water was available. These collected dust and germs, or were flyblown and used without rinsing day after day. Most men had not bathed or laundered their clothes since leaving Bataan, some as long as three weeks before. Dirt, grime, etc. was caked on all of us. Our clothes were stiff with and smelled of three weeks of sweating under a tropical sun. Unshaved whiskers and long hair were germ catchers with the three weeks growth. I was fortunate enough to catch the water detail one day and on the last trip to the river, the Jap guard let us get in the river, clothes and all. It sure did feel good. I don't know how clean I got, but for a couple of days afterwards, I did not smell myself.

The latrines were built too close to the living quarters and were nothing but straddle trenches, leaving as much on the outside as in the trench. With lumber from the scrap heap, A-frames were built and the trenches were made wider and deeper, but these were not changed often enough to keep the flies from breeding and being a constant pest both while trying to eat and trying to cook. These were big green blowflies you have to beat off to keep them from taking over your food. A little slack lime would have taken care of the problem but the Jap didn't seem to care one way or the other. There was a strong feeling among them that we deserved no better.

Try explaining to someone who never lived under such conditions how dehumanizing it is. Sick, many with malaria, diarrhea, and dysentery – any one of which would be bad enough, but put the three together along with fever, chills, sweating, and running to the latrine every 15 minutes day in and day out - not feeling like eating, does not leave much reason for living. Then there are the complainers, the ones who never miss a chow line but are too sick to take care of their personal needs. If you were fortunate as I was, half-able to be up and around, you volunteered for any detail that got you outside the camp area. Digging graves and toting water was hard work, but it was better than staying in camp and seeing and smelling…yes, enduring the misery inside. I didn't want to get caught up in that degradation and not be able to get out. There was never any doubt in my mind but that I would get back to civilization one day

The men who arrived early in Camp O'Donnell became the funeral detail. About a hundred of us were turned out each morning and marched to a field designated the cemetery. We were divided into groups of 16 to 20 and, with shovels and picks, we were ordered to dig holes six feet wide, 12 feet long and 4 feet deep. The ground in dry season like it was now, was dry and hard clay, almost like concrete. We took turns picking and shoveling until the hole had reached it proper dimension, then we were marched back inside to eat watery lugao made from boiled rice with boiled camotes (sweet potatoes), and take a short rest before the burial detail that afternoon, when the bodies of those who had died in the past 24 hours were carried out for burial.

The evening burial detailed consisted, for the most part, of the same group that had dug the graves that morning. Each body was stripped of all clothing, placed on a sawali mat probably two feet by 6 ft., mounted on a frame the same size, with two poles running down the sides and extending a foot past each end so that four men could lift and carry the litter on their shoulders, which meant if there were 50 dead bodies there had to be 200 men to carry them. And they were dying by that number and sometimes more, every day I was there. At the gravesite, ten bodies were placed side-by-side in each grave and covered. The American officer or Chaplain, who accompanied the burial detail, usually said a few words and kept a report of who was placed in each grave. Then we went back to camp, to repeat the same thing the next day.

Before any organization was set up in O'Donnell, a sick man had to make the best of it. If he had a buddy to bring him chow and carry water for him, he was lucky. If you caught a malaria chill or were stricken with dysentery until you became a mere shadow of yourself, you took care of yourself or died where you lay.

Because of this, what remained of the Medical Corps began to organize some sort of hospital where a man could make sick call and there would be someone to offer him sympathy, which was about all he would get as there was very little medicine. What was available was brought in by thoughtful corpsmen or by doctors in their Red Cross kits. Many of the men, before capture, had gone to one of the two hospitals in Bataan and picked up bottles of sulfa drugs, quinine and other much needed medicines, thinking they'd need them later. A lot of these men gave their medicines to the medical corps to be used for those who most needed them; others, however, kept them for their own use or sold them at outlandish prices on the black market. All of us, at some time, probably did something we are not exactly proud of, but this act of selling medicines that were so badly needed, in my opinion, was about the lowest of the low.

The fact that about one-third of the Americans in O'Donnell were down with one of the big three diseases and many of their able-bodied buddies were on one detail or another, leaving the sick to manage for themselves, is how Col. Sage (later General), the commanding officer of the camp, was able to convince the Japanese hierarchy that some place ought to be set aside for the sick to be hospitalized.

The old headquarters for the Philippine units, who had been there, was designated as a hospital area. The Medics all moved there and began trying to take care of the worst cases in spite of the shortage of medical supplies. At least, the buildings were in better shape than our barracks. Two days later, the Jap erected a fence around this building and the sickest were moved to these new quarters. A separate kitchen was set up for the hospital and some able-bodied men and cooks were moved there to assist in the handling of the patients.

As the days wore by, more and more men were stricken and taken to the hospital area. Conditions were no better in the main camp. I would dare say half the population was incapacitated to the point of being unable to do little but feed their own selves. The Japanese kept calling for more and more details to do this and do that. It was almost impossible to find men to do the grave detail and bury the dead, and we were loosing forty to fifty men a day. The Filipinos, who were billeted in another part of the camp, were carrying out a 100 to 150 a day; but then, there were more of them interned than Americans. It was rumored but not confirmed, that Americans were dying faster because they were not accustomed to the oriental diet. So many died, the hospital became known as the "Zero Ward," because only a few who entered ever returned to duty side.

Vicious rumors were circulated that doctors and corpsmen were eating all the chow and starving the patients, that corpsmen were robbing the patients of their belongings. This was highly unlikely because most of us didn't have anything worth stealing. Patients were kicked and cuffed around and not properly tended - too weak to move, were left to wallow in their excrement, eventually dying in it. Many more were the rumors circulating in the main camp.

How many of these rumors were true, I can't say. An idle and sick mind can become vicious. I believe most of these rumors were figments of those sick minds, but there could have been a little bit of truth to them, because they say 'where there is smoke there has to be fire.' It wasn't impossible to believe some these stories after having seen 'corpsmen' selling drugs and medicines in the main camp. But while I was on the burial detail, the hospital served as a mortuary and this was where we picked up the bodies for burial, and I did not see any such treatment or act of brutality. From my observation, these men were getting the best treatment that was available for the limited facilities with which the doctors and corpsmen had to work

On the first grave detail I worked, there were 10 men. We dug a grave for two men who died the night before. Before the week was over, there were forty men on the detail, and by the end of the second week, there were eighty. When I left O'Donnell June 1, 1941, two hundred men were going out each day for burials. The most men who ever died in any 24-hour period, was sixty-four (64).

The grave detail was divided into two sections when we first started: the group who dug the graves in the morning and the group who carried the bodies out in the afternoon and covered them. As more men became sick and unable to do this hard work, the detail became one unit, digging the graves in the morning and returning in the afternoon to do the burial. This became a very large detail of more that 200 men, with the death rate at between 40 and 50 a day, and four men to a litter to carry a body, 200 men was not too many, especially working in the type of clay-like soil in which the graves were dug. All this made for a long days work.

Each grave, as I said, had room for 10 bodies laid side by side, and each one was marked with the name, serial number and position of each man denoted in the grave. Or so we were told. But in our physically and mentally fatigued state, I could have sworn the bodies were just tossed in and covered up.

After the graves were dug, we returned to camp for the noon meal of rice and thin vegetable soup and a short rest before being called out again for the afternoon burial ceremony. During the day, the corpsmen and doctors had to place the dead bodies in what was dubbed the mortuary - a large isolated room away from the hospital area. Here we stripped he body of all clothing and footwear. This amounted to nothing more than a g-string and maybe a ragged shirt or a pair of cut-off dungarees. Shoes had already been removed if there had been any. This was not a pleasant task, as many of the men had died of dysentery or malaria and were sometimes covered with fecal matter. A little Vicks would have come in handy on many occasions.

On these sawali the bodies were placed, and in Indian style procession the bodies were carried to the gravesite, deposited there, and a short prayer said by the accompanying Chaplain. Then the graves were filled and tamped, and we returned to the mortuary with the empty litters and back to the camp enclosure to wait for another day of the same.

While I was on this detail, I came down with a Malaria attack. We were coming in from our morning chore of digging the graves for the afternoon burial. I started feeling sort of dizzy, but thought it was because I was thirsty and had no more water in my canteen. Before I could get to my bunking area, I started feeling like I was freezing, and a few seconds later, started shaking. I filled my canteen and took a deep drink of water. Then, because I started chilling harder, I wrapped my blanket around me. That didn't help a bit. I shook so badly and ached all over. One of my buddies came back from chow with his mess kit, to eat where we always ate and, noting my shaking, asked what was wrong. Hell, I had never experienced anything like this in my life. He called an old 31st infantryman Sergeant over who did not mince words. "You got Malaria," he said. "I've had it many times. You think you are going to die and sometime hope you do. But hang in there, drink lots of water and sweat it out." The chills lasted until my fever peaked, then I started drinking water, trying to put out the fire burning inside. When the fever finally broke, I learned what the old Sarge was taking about when he said 'sweat it out.' A medic had come by while I was chilling and told me that as soon as the fever broke I should stay wrapped up in the blanket. That was hard to do. I wanted to get out of all my clothes, but I did as he told me. When the fever dropped to normal, I quit sweating. My blanket and clothes were so wet you could have wrung water out of them. Fortunately, my buddy got my noon chow for me, because by this time I was so hungry I could have eaten most anything. I devoured it and felt as if nothing had ever happened, except it left me a little weak. The whole episode lasted about 2 and half or three hours. By this time, the burial detail had been called back to work. I was afraid I would get in trouble with the Jap, but the old Sarge said not to worry. All the Jap wanted was numbers anyway. To them, we all looked alike. "You are not going to be going back out for some time if I am any judge of Malaria," he said. "Lets just hope we can get you some quinine."

He was right. It was ten days before I was able to do anything but get up and get my food and eat it. There was no quinine available, so I sweated out the ten days of those chills and fever. The attacks seemed to hit at the same time each day and last for about the same length of time. By the eleventh day, I was getting worried because I didn't know how long I could last at the rate I was going. The morning moved along slowly and as the usual time arrived…strangely, I did not get the usual forerunner indications an attack was coming. When the grave detail came in for lunch, I still had not had an attack. I sat around with my buddies I worked with and as we ate, commented on the fact that I was able to have the noon meal with them A couple of hours later they went back out and I was still free from an attack. Night came and went, another day passed, another night and still no Malaria.

After three days, the old Sarge called me one lucky dude because I had beaten the Malaria without any quinine. The next day he had me on the water detail, hauling water from the well for kitchen use. The water detail was lighter work than all that digging. I never got put back on the burial detail, but did catch most all the other details at one time or another. Just as I was getting ready to make a Bataan detail, the old Malaria kicked me in the butt again, but I was only down three days this time.

By now the camp had long been reorganized with all units together. Old Sarge had gone with his 31st infantry group, but I remembered what he said and sweated it out. Funny, I never knew his name or heard him called anything but Sarge, but I will always remember him. I had two or three more attacks after we got to Cabanatuan, but not one of them over three days duration. I was given quinine with one of them and never had an attack the next day. Like I say 'que sera, sera.'

Our conditions and our death rate was deplorable, but among the 50,000 Filipinos who surrendered, imprisoned in another section of the post, conditions were even more deplorable, and they were dropping like flies before a sprayer. They had little or no organization among themselves, and lived even worse... drinking polluted water from the river without boiling it first, eating half cooked food and urinating and excreting any place that happened to strike their fancy or when they felt the urge. From what we heard, no efforts were made to dig latrines or take any of the precautions necessary for sanitation. Due to these despairing conditions, at times as many as 200 or more bodies were counted as they filed by our camp on the way to their own cemetery.

This was the hellhole that had swallowed us up. To say that is was hell, almost negates the word "Hell". To say that men could and did exist under such horrendous circumstances seems unfathomable, but we who did survive and in a large part, forgotten the worst, still remember and find it difficult to answer the one unanswerable question, 'Why?' 'Why me?'

I am not a learned scholar or philosopher nor am I all that intelligent, but over the years I find myself dwelling on the fate of all those men who were imprisoned at O'Donnell and later Cabanatuan and I always come back to that question 'Why Me?' Why did I survive? We were all in the same age classification, all products of the American way of life. For the past five months being subjected to the same conditions, drinking the same water, eating the same food, incurring and suffering from the same diseases, yet some died of those maladies while others lived to tell about it. Why? Why? Why? A question I have asked myself a thousand times. To watch two men lying side by side in the Zero ward, sick of dysentery and malaria, obviously of the same stature physically, sick for the same length of time, eating when possible, the same thing and generally both equally as sick as the other, one dies, the other lives.

Case in point is a friend of mine who called himself "a washed out priest." He came down with Malaria, chilling so badly he shook the flimsy barracks. Day after day he was fever ravaged and racked by chills. There was no quinine. Yet he threw it off and later went out on details; then, plagued with diarrhea for weeks, pulled out of it and again returned to work. Then he suffered a second attack of malaria, this time the cerebral type, and he died in a screaming coma. Why?

Do they get tired and just give up? Is there such a thing as giving up? Did one man engage in a cleaner lifestyle when he was younger? I don't know, but I don't think so. I have seen men whom I knew to have dissipated all their lives get sick with all the usual tropical diseases and regain their health, get sick again and finally make it back home, so it couldn't be the lifestyle. Could it be that some were more religious than others? Again, I don't know. But I have known men who were outwardly very religious, dying, while others not so pious lived on. Maybe it's a mind thing.

There were two men from my outfit, good buddies, lying side by side in the Zero ward. Both men were in their prime, both had been 200 pounds of hard muscle, although by now they were a far cry from that. More like 120 pounds. They were good men, dependable and outgoing. Both ate the same food, got the same bit of medicine we were able to rake and scrape for them. The only difference in the two I could find was that one was married with a little boy three years old and the other was single. The married one died and the other returned to live out his life in his home in New Mexico.

Why the family man? Surely he didn't just give up. Look what he had to live for, but I want to say he gave up. We talked to him, we begged and pleaded with him to eat. We bought canned food on the black market for him but he just wouldn't eat. He wouldn't even try. The priest met with him, but could get nowhere. Then one day not long before he died, after hundreds of times telling him all the reasons he had to live, he made this statement: "My wife and kid will be better off when I am gone. I have $10,000 government insurance and $25,000 civilian insurance. They will get it all." Right there, I thought I had it. Death is all in the mind. Sometimes a man just gives up.

He just gets tired of fighting and it is so easy, after battling so long to stay alive, to lie back and pass away. It relieves ones body and mind of all the pain and worrying fatigue. There, I think is the answer to it all, but I'm just guessing. I can't possible know what actually was going on in this man's mind, nor can anyone else, so I am back to square one. I had an experience of my own where this query came up, related later in this book. 'Que sera, sera.' What is to be will be.

Other than being enclosed behind a barbed-wire fence and Jap guards walking the outside the camp, our camp was run much like any Army camp.. General King, who surrendered Bataan to the Nips, naturally took complete command of the camp and organized it into various units that were on Battan, and assembled us as such. The 200th and 515th CAC were unified under one command with Col. Sage, Adjutant General of the New Mexico National Guard again in charge.

After General Kings' arrival in camp and a complete reorganization, he made the rounds of the various units, explaining the conditions and legalities of the surrender, all in a short, inspiring, non oratorical speech. The content and feeling behind it made us remember it. One thing that stands out in my mind until today was hearing him say: "You did not surrender, I surrendered you."

In those seven words, one man sacrificed himself and took the blame for the bungling of hundreds of men higher up, both in the Philippines and the United States. He assumed the responsibility for the laxity and pacifism of a whole nation. In those seven words, General King became a hero to every last man that had fought on Bataan, because in so doing he took upon himself a great burden, whether he knew it or not at the time. That is what his statement amounted to.

Why weren't the Philippines better defended? Why did the Jap make a sneak play on Pearl Harbor? Why didn't we know about the eminent danger of the Jap? The Filipinos knew. Why were raw recruits, guardsmen, and reserves sent to the Philippines at this time? Why? Why? Why? These questions were supposed to have been threshed out after the Japanese surrender in August 1945, but to my knowledge, no blame was ever established…leaving General King to carry it all to his grave. If he was not a martyr, General King was a 20th century facsimile.

General King remained in O'Donnell until, along with the other Generals from Battan and Corriegdor, they surrendered May 9, 1942, when they were shipped out to Formosa and later to Manchuria. Later on, all senior grade officers, Colonels, Lt. Colonel and Majors were shipped out, rumored to Manchuria.

As the camp became more organized, most details became self-serving details. That is, they were for our own survival. The wood hauling detail furnished wood for the kitchen. The rice hauling detail and cooks helpers were both survival crews. There were some 25 men who kept the pumps and water department running smoothly. Latrines crews were picked each day to cover old latrines and dig new ones. Police call every morning involved all able-bodied men to go through the camp, picking up trash and keeping the grounds clean cut down the fly population.

The only detail not stationed in O'Donnell and having no connection with the camp was a 200-man telephone crew picked from the camp to erect a line from Capas to the Japanese Headquarters there. Many other permanent details were picked from the camp and sent to different parts of the island and to other islands in the Philippine group. One group went to Baguio to build roads, another to Clark Field to fix up and extend the runway. One big detail I almost got on was sent back into Bataan to clean up all the guns, trucks, and ammunition still remaining in the jungle where they were left when Bataan surrendered. A malaria attack kept me off that detail. When they returned to Cabanatuan, I was told that it was a good detail. Hard work, but they were fed well and allowed to shop in the barrios and buy extra food with the money they were paid.

Toward the end of May, rainy season started. Most of the barracks, as I said earlier, were fragile at best and leaked like a sieve. Many of the men slept under the barracks on the damp ground instead of the wet, too-crowded inside. The Latrines overflowed and the contents spread everywhere. The following day, the sun came out and hoards of flies were swarming everywhere, blowing the feces throughout the camp The stench was almost more than a body could stand when the ground started steaming under the tropical sun. Then the rain would come and the atmosphere would be clean for a short while.

The kitchens had very little shelter over them. The cooks had to shut down when a rain shower came up. Fires were quenched in the downpour, making it almost impossible to start again with the wet wood. Sometimes it was as late as 10 o'clock at night before the evening meal was served. Rain dripped in on the raw rice causing it to mold, which gave it a bitter taste when cooked…still, it was better than nothing.

The one redeeming thing about the rains, we could take a bath. You could do it one of two ways - with or without your clothes. Just step out under the eaves of the roof of the barracks and you had as good a shower as you could ask for. While you showered, you could be washing your clothes. When you finished, you pulled off what clothes you had. (most of us still had shorts) and wait for the sun came out and dry them. You could stay wearing your shorts and letting them dry on you. It really did not make much difference, as there would be another rain the next day. You stayed wet most of the time anyway, and it was nice to be something other than sweating for a change.

Such were the conditions when the Jap issued orders that O'Donnell would be evacuated except for those who absolutely were physically unable to travel, and the doctors, corpsmen and few personnel necessary to take care of cooking, etc. Thus we found ourselves, some 800 strong, strung out early on the morning of June 1, 1942, marching into Capas to catch trains for Cabanatuan.

There was plenty of speculation about our new home. Many of the old fellows who had been in the islands for a long time, said it was a lot better camp. Others said it was not better than what we were leaving. Some painted a bright picture while others painted a dark one. We will see.

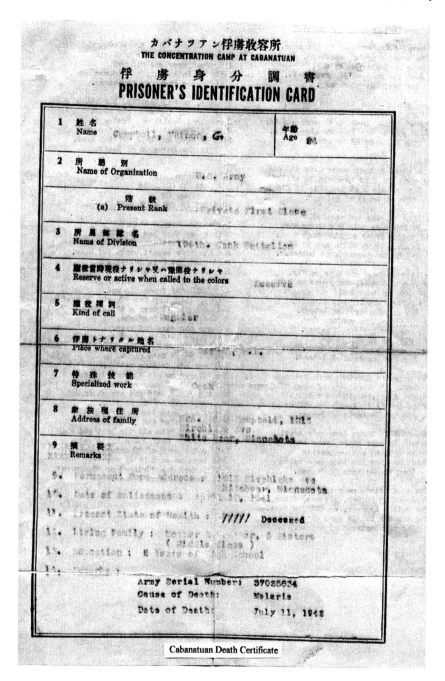

Japanese Death Certificate

Clemens A. Kathman

CHAPTER FOUR
CABANATUAN JUNE 2, 1942--SEPT. 18, 1943

I have heard many stories of horror that took place at O'Donnell after I left, but have never been able to get a true picture of what happened to those left there, too sick to take care of themselves. I know there is a Memorial marker set up where the graveyard was at that time, because I have seen pictures of it. Many versions of the aftermath and eventual demise of the camp have been related over the past 60 years, and I suppose there may be some truth in all or most of them.

This trip was the reverse of the trip in. We walked back to Capas, crowded into the boxcars and traveled under the same conditions as when we came in. After a 12 hour train ride, packed 50 men to a car, the sun beating down with all its fury and with sweat pouring off us like an open faucet; add to that sick men vomiting, others with dysentery or diarrhea, hearing the call in the floor under our feet, the only place available. We arrived and detrained in Cabanatuan, the second largest city on the island of Luzon.

We were marched over to a schoolhouse and bedded down for the night on the damp ground surrounding it, and given a ration of rice and onion soup. Tired after such a hectic and debilitating day, all of us hit the ground and we slept, in spite of the hardness and dampness of the ground.

The next morning we started the five-mile walk to the POW camp. It had been a Philippine Army training center, housing an infantry outfit and a couple of Field Artillery regiments. From a distance, it looked much the same as O'Donnell, but given a closer look, we found it more substantial and cleaner. It was completely surrounded by a tall barbed wire fence. The area outside of the fence was dotted with 15 to 20 foot guard towers, situated 100 or so feet apart, surrounding the complex. A large gate opened into the middle section, which served as the Japanese headquarters and had originally served as a drill field for the Filipinos training there. On each side of the middle section, separated by barbed-wire fences, were the barrack areas. We were marched into the section on the left side, and assigned barracks. At that time, the area on the right remained empty, but as more prisoners were moved in and the sick list kept growing, it was used as a hospital.

The barracks, although similar to those at O'Donnell, were sturdier and cleaner. They were approximately the same size, 16-feet wide and 30-feet in length, two tiered with bamboo slats for sleeping. They were lined up in three rows each three barracks deep, with the front barrack acting as a kitchen and storage. The other two built with two-tiered bunks running down each side were spaced some 20 feet apart with a latrine area 50 or so feet in the rear. Each barracks housed 60 men and each kitchen fed the units, 120 men, three meals a day (such as they were). Water spigots were available for each unit of kitchen and barracks. An A-frame latrine was situated about 50 ft behind each unit. An open space of probably 50 yards separated the barracks from the barbed wire fence surrounding the entire compound. This was declared to be a 'no man's land.' No one was allowed past the latrines unless accompanied by a Jap guard.

The grounds were higher than the surrounding terrain, so drainage was far better than O'Donnell. Immediately after being assigned barracks, bolos were issued and the cogon grass that had grown up around the barracks was cleaned out, thus eliminating breeding grounds for mosquitoes. Others were put to work digging new latrines and covering the ones used earlier by the Filipinos. We hoped to profit from the mistakes made at O'Donnell.

In spite of the many spigots dotting the area, until the second pump could be repaired and pressed into service, water was rationed, but never to the extent we found in the departed compound. For the first time we could bathe, wash clothes and have plenty of water for cooking. Later on, Camp #3 Cabantuan, where the Corriegdor prisoners were taken, was moved to Camp #1 and more wells were dug, to take care of the influx and extend service to the hospital area.

The kitchens were similar to those at O'Donnell, but in much better condition. There was a roof over the cooking areas to eliminate the problems encountered at O'Donnel of drowning out the fires when it rained. There was more equipment, later supplemented by mess equipment picked up in Bataan and brought into camp for use. In spite of all this, the chow situation took a turn for the worse instead of better, as we had hoped.

Among other things brought in from Bataan was clothing and blankets. Not enough at first to go around but by the end of July most every man had a blanket and a change of clothes. So many men died, their belongings were cleaned and sterilized to supplement the clothing shortage. Most everyone had something suitable to eat out of. Many men were coming in off details in Bataan, Baguio, Clark Field, and other places, bringing things they'd bought, stolen, found or had given them outside. One could almost always find a buddy who fixed him up if need be, for a small price.

As I mentioned earlier, Cabanatuan Camp #1 had two sections and the middle section had once been a drill field. In this area, the Japanese built their headquarters, moving buildings from as far away as a mile or more. To do this, they would take a couple hundred men or as many as could get around the building and by brute force lift it up and move it to the new site. I have no idea how many houses were moved in by his method. They even dug up a 40-foot tree with a 6-foot root ball on it, and with as many men as could get a hold on it, carried it at least a quarter of a mile and set it out in a hole dug by another crew. Believe it or not, the tree lived and I don't think it even wilted. They had crews working all the time beautifying the landscape. The Japanese section was clean and well landscaped.

In the area on the other side of the drill field, the barracks were left vacant, but were later utilized as a hospital area, as by the middle of July so many were still dying and sick and needed to be isolated. Considering the starvation diet we were placed on, the best you could hope for was not to get sick. Once that happened there was only one way you could go, down. After a POW was reduced to the point where he was unable to get his food, he was sent to the hospital area. This area was opened, cleaned up and doctors and corpsmen set up shop. Later, the equipment from Hospital #1 on Bataan was moved into the area, but all this equipment was useless without medicine and the Japanese still were not making any effort to relieve that situation. They were systematically eliminating all of us while claiming they were adhering to the Geneva pact for POW treatment. It was not what they were doing, but what they were not doing that was killing us.

Just before Christmas of 1942, the Red Cross was finally allowed admittance, but not until after another twelve to fifteen hundred men had died of starvation and disease. I don't say the food the Jap supplied was any better after the Red Cross visit, but several hundred head of carabao donated by the Catholic Church reached the camp and that added a little protein to the diet. Christmas 1942 saw Red Cross boxes being issued, one to each man. They were from Britain, Canada and South Africa Red Cross. They all contained basically the same items: corned beef, sugar, cocoa, hardtack, dried milk, Spam, coffee, chocolate bars, tins of potted meat, orange concentrate, mutton, marmalade, jams, cheese, raisins, dried prunes, oleo, butter and other foods stuffs common to each of the sources.

Coming at Christmas, the Red Cross boxes were a psychological stimulus for all the prisoners. The contents were short lived for some while others strung out the tasty morsels to enhance the regular ration doled out by the Japanese. In these boxes, there was not enough food to make a lot of difference in the physical condition of the men, but with the South African boxes came a big shipment of bulk foodstuff and much needed medicine, and the Carabao donated by the Catholic church all helped to turn the death rate around by half in a matter of only a couple of months.

Until the Red Cross made their visit and Camp #3 and Camp #1 were consolidated into one camp, the death rate was averaging 50 to 60 a day, due to the Japanese' incessant demands for more work and less food from the already sick and diseased prisoners. It was pretty plain their overall plan was to get everything they could out of the POWs at the least expense before they were forced into mass graves. The Geneva Convention be damned.

About the first of 1943, with the aid of the Red Cross food, the death rate started to drop. About that same time, a work crew opened a big gate in the back fence. This took several days - conjectures rampant as to its purpose. It didn't take long to find out. As soon as the gate was finished, two trucks brought loads of shovels, bolos, picks, grubbing hoes, hoes and most every type of farm implements imaginable.

The next day all able-bodied men not already assigned to the burial, wood chopping, grave-digging or other details, were assembled in front of their respective barracks and informed that we were starting a farm. We were going to be self-sustaining. We would have so many hectares of rice paddies, so many hectares of vegetables, sweet potatoes, corn, and so on, but first the land had to be cleared of cogon grass, then the roots dug up, cultivated, watered and gleaned when ready. Every man able to get to the farm would do his part. This was a community thing for the communal good of all involved.

Then the gates were opened and as the men filed through, they were given an implement for chopping, digging or raking. Those who did not have implements would be bearers. We were lined up elbow-to-elbow in a line that stretched for 200 or 300 yards. Those with bolos started whacking at the tough cogon grass. and as the grass fell, it was picked up by the bearers and stacked in a big pile in the rear to be burned later. The men with grubbing hoes, hoes and picks followed behind and dug up the grass roots. These also were stacked and burned. This went on until the whole area surrounding the camp was completely devoid of grass. Some estimated the total ground cleared at two sections or more. That is 1320 acres.

After the area was cleared, there still remained dozens of giant anthills, some 6-feet tall or more and three to four feet in diameter. With the assistance of picks, shovels, hoes and rakes, these were torn down and broken into small pieces and spread out over the landscape. The produce planted where these anthills had been was much bigger, more lush and productive than that grown on the surrounding soil.

I Was There, Charley

While one group of men was planting and watering the small plants as they sprouted, another large group was forming up rice paddies. This was a backbreaking job. The area was laid out in 20x20-foot plots during the rainy season of 1943. Embankments dividing each plot were constructed by pilling mud along the lines of the plot until it was above the water. Most of this work was done bending over and to this day, my back starts hurting when I think about it. Ouch!

After the plots were all laid out, then came the planting. Rice had been thickly planted in beds earlier and were, by now, some 12 to 14 inches high. These rice plants were then pulled from the beds and singly inserted along a heavy cord, 20 foot long, where, earlier, knots about 12 inches apart had been tied to mark the spot where the plant was to be inserted. Two men on each side of the paddy stood on the ridge, and extended the cord between them as ten men with rice plants positioned themselves an equal distance apart in the water beside the line. Where there was a knot in the string, beneath it was a plant, planted in the mud. Each of the ten men planted two plants, then the two men on the bank moved the string a foot and the same procedure was repeated, the line moved again and so on until the plot was covered. In any direction you looked, the plants were all in line. I did not get to stay in the Philippines long enough to see the product of my labor, but I still feel it.

The remainder of the farm was planted in all types of native vegetables. One of them being okra, which grew to the height well above my 6 feet, with pods 10 to 12 inches long. Cucumbers grew up to 18 inches long. squash, eggplant, and other native vegetables flourished in this virgin soil turned over by the sweat of thousands of Japanese POWs. Water was carried from a nearby creek in buckets strung by a strong cord from a bamboo pole resting on the carriers shoulder. A lot of water can be moved by 500 men in an endless chain, carrying 2 buckets of water on a pole suspended from a rope.

After the farm started producing, more and more veggies started showing up in the mess kit. The tender end of sweet potato vines make delicious greens and takes nothing from the growth of the potato. By the time the farm was really producing on a large scale, the Jap called up some 800 men to be sent to Japan in September of 1943. I was in that group. I've often wondered who took care of the farm. You take 800 men out of a work force and something's got to give.

By the time we were moved to Cabanatuan, most of us had not shaved nor had a haircut since days before becoming prisoners. We looked like refugees from the house of David. As soon as a pair of clippers became available, I had my first haircut and shave. I was disappointed in not having a mirror to see myself in the wild, but all I had to do was look at the man next to me and use my imagination. It was not a pleasing sight. We used clippers and kept our head and face clipped as close as possible after that. It was easier to keep clean and more hygienic. Of course, during the rainy season you didn't have to worry where you would be taking a bath...just step out under the eaves and let nature do the honors.

If I remember right, the first detail I was placed on was the wood cutting detail. There were at least 6 to 8 kitchens on the work side of the camp that needed wood. These stoves, or open pits where the Kawa pots sat, needed large amounts of chopped wood to feed their blazing maw. In these pots all food was cooked and fires burned almost 24 hours a day. The detail was made up of two sections. The first section was the ones who went out in the morning with a small sack lunch into the woods to spend the day cutting down trees to be used as firewood. The second section chopped the trees into large pieces to be transported into camp. A third group stayed in camp and reduced the logs into firewood to fit in the furnace. This last detail was a permanent one, the same men working it every day in the same kitchen. It was composed of large, muscular men who were fed extra so they would be able to do the job day in and day out.

The men who felled the trees (native growth at least eight inches in diameter) worked in groups of three, one chopping while the other two rested, taking turns so we could work all day without falling on our faces from fatigue. The other group chopped the tree into five or six foot logs, stripped them of the smaller limbs and carried them out to where the trucks were waiting to take them back into camp. There were usually 100 men or more on this detail.

A lot of the time, as the area where we were chopping was heavily forested and made almost impassable because of the undergrowth, much time was spent clearing out these low growing bushes so we could get in to fell the larger trees. So a larger group of men was sent out to clear the underbrush. In many of these cases, the trucks were unable to get in close enough, and the wood had to be carried, sometimes as far as a quarter mile to the trucks. This made for more backbreaking work as a green log, 6 ft long and 8 or 10 inches in diameter, might weight 200 or 300 pounds. Many times only three or four men were used to carry a log of this size.

With a proper diet we could have maintained our weight and health, but as it was, a lot of the weaker men lost so much weight they started dropping within an hour or two after starting work. I was down to 135 pounds from the 175 I weighed on Dec. 8 1942 when the war started. After three weeks, I began to think I was having another malaria attack. I would be chopping away at the trunk of a tree and suddenly feel dizzy and a cold chill sort of shake me. Then it would come my time to rest and by the time it was my time to chop again, I would feel better. This went on for a couple of weeks until one morning we were working on a real tall tree with limbs starting 30 of so feet up the trunk, the sun beating down unmercifully, and I felt the chill coming. In five minutes I was shaking like a leaf. The Japanese guard saw something was wrong and thought I was faking it and prodded me with the butt of his rifle, knocking me off my feet. I just lay there shaking so hard it hurt all over. The last I remember, I thought I saw the Jap running off. The guys I was working with told me later that he was scared and thought I was having some sort of seizure. When my fever went as high as it was going, I came out of it and felt extremely hot, my ears ringing like mad and my throat as dry as a desert floor. Someone had moved me into the shade of a small tree. I reached for my canteen, opened and took a deep swallow and almost vomited it. I looked around for my crew. They were some 50 or 75 yards away working on another tree. The Jap guard was standing under a tree about halfway between my buddies and me. He ambled over and looked me up and down, then reached down and felt my forehead. He shook his hand and uttered something like "domei" which in Japanese means 'bad, and walked back to his spot under the tree. As it had done before, the fever broke and I started sweating.

The guys downed their tree and the Jap motioned them to follow him as they all gathered around me and sat down. The Jap looked at his watch and then sat down himself. He took out a cigarette and lit it. The other guys asked me how I was feeling and made small talk. I guess we must have sat there for 30 or 45 minutes when the Guard motioned us to get our tools and we headed down hill to the road and the trucks. It was quitting time. Soon the other crews came in, we loaded up and went back to camp, grateful for the almost hour rest the guard had given us. My buddies said that after I passed out, he might have gone to see what he should do. Maybe 20 minutes later, he came back and looked at me for several minutes, finally getting up enough nerve to feel of me in spite of the shaking. Turning, sort of in a questioning way, he said 'Mararia. (The Japanese can't pronounce an 'L.') They told him yes and motioned them to put me in the shade and ordered them back to work. We decided there was, maybe, one compassionate Nip. I made sick call and given a couple of quinine tablets and told to stay in camp a couple of days. I never worked the wood detail again. For small favors I was most thankful, although I heard they did start feeding the men who worked the wood detail, extra food.

This Malaria attack lasted four days. The Medics gave me two quinine tablets each day. I had one other attack in late July and early August, which lasted five days. Sometime in early 1943 I had what I thought was Malaria, but I did not have the chills, just ran a high fever. The medics said it sounded like Dengue Fever and had me drink lots of water. After five days, the fever subsided and a day or two later I was back at the old grind.

After I got over the Malaria attack in the woods, I was assigned to the burial detail, this time on the digging part of it. Just as in O'Donnell, the graves were dug 6-feet wide, 12-feet long and 4-feet deep. The soil in the middle valley of Luzon is sandy and made the digging much easier than in the foothills of the land around O'Donnell. Here we only used picks in the final foot of clay-like structured soil. The guards on this detail were much rougher than those on the wood cutting detail, because the work was much nearer the headquarters and subject to unsuspected visits from the Japanese hierarchy; thus the guards were constantly pushing and prodding to keep the POWs at work. A good thing was that as soon as we had the allotted graves dug, we went back into camp. This was not so bad until they decided that the grave-digging detail, with a few extra men, could dig the graves and then in the afternoon, like at O'Donnell, carry the bodies to the grave site and bury them. They didn't miss a thing.

Well, at least we got a good two hours break in between digging the graves and doubling back to bury the bodies. The same procedures as at O'Donnell were adhered to at Cabanatuan and became pretty much routine.

Some interesting incidents broke up the monotony now then. Incidents of near catastrophic mishaps that, under other circumstances and in other places would have been a serious matter. But times and places change everything, and these were trying times and unfortunate places.

One such incident happened on the way to the grave area. The cemetery plot was a half-mile from the zero ward in the hospital. On this quiet, hot, still day we were plodding along, four men to a litter, probably as many as 35 or 40 liters, when the arm of a corpse which had been crossed over the other before starting the trek, due to the up and down movement of the litter and gradually yielding to the force of gravity, slipped on the side of the litter, right in the face of a Navajo Indian bearer. Imagine for one moment walking along and having an arm dangling in front of your nose. What would be your reaction? This Indian dropped his corner of the litter and took off like Hogans's Goat, with three or four Jap guards after him. The part of the procession in front of the accident kept moving, but the rear part came to a screeching halt. Fortunately, the Chaplain who was accompanying the procession stepped up, directed the men to put the corpse back on the litter and took the corner abandoned by the Indian and off we went to catch up with the first part of the funeral party, only without four Jap Guards and one scared Indian.

When rainy season started in earnest, we couldn't finish the graves and get the bodies back to them in the afternoon before the graves were half full of water. In this sort of situation it is impossible to bail the water out of a hole that big. As the corpses were placed in the grave, they would float. They had to be held down until sufficient dirt could be shoveled in to hold them in place. On one such occasion, as one body was pushed under and dirt was being piled in, up popped a head demanding to know where his shoes were. He was pulled out and taken back to the hospital. He had cerebral malaria and in a coma. The medics, not denoting any pulse, declared him dead. The supposition was that when he hit that cold rainwater, it shocked him back to consciousness. I heard he "really died" the next day.

The grave detail was a gruesome job, but in the daily operation of a camp as big as this one, it was a job that had to be done and someone had to do it. I was almost glad when I came down with a case of Dengue Fever. I first thought it was another attack of Malaria, but medics diagnosed it as Dengue. I did not have the chills with it, but did have fever and I ached all over to the point of almost crying. I took aspirin for a couple of days and drank lots of water, then returned to duty, this time in the Japanese kitchen across the road from our barracks.

This chore did not last very long, but long enough to get a birds eye view of the Jap in his natural habitat. This was an officers' kitchen, whereas we had only mingled with the enlisted personnel. In this kitchen, Jap cooks supervised and did the cooking and were the equivalent of a sergeant in the USA army. We did the dirty work, such as peeling, dicing, slicing, cutting up and, of course, all around cleanup. It was hard but rewarding work. We ate what was served in the officer's mess…not much, but varied and more substantial.

The only drawback about this job was, while we were supposed to be wrestling targets for the Japanese cooks, at the end of the day when the work was over and it was time to play, they used us as guinea pigs in an arena outside the kitchen. They liked to practice their Judo and such and got a big kick out of picking one of us who was tall, and knocking or throwing us to the ground. I don't know what would have happened if one of us used the old hard knuckles and gave one of them a punch in the face. We didn't try to find out, we just took the blows and kicks and blocked them off as best we could. We did not dare get offensive with them.

On one occasion, the Japanese hierarchy entertained a group of high-up officials, really putting on the dog. Several hundred pound of Loppa-Loppa, a species of the tuna family, was brought into camp and we spent the day slicing it in thin slices and, along with thin sliced daikon and cucumbers, stacked them in a crock jar, layer after layer, and covering it with sugar laden soy-sauce. Sound appetizing? At the time, this raw fish and veggie dish tasted pretty good, but now I attribute my gastronomical craving to a starved and hungry stomach. The Japanese officers must have considered it a tasty morsel, as attested to by the empty crock jars and drained sake bottles.

A few days later, I developed an extremely sore throat, which finally got so sore I made sick call. The medic took one look at it and immediately sent me to the hospital isolation ward. The doctor in the isolation ward checked my admittance sheet and I caught a glance of the word 'diphtheria.' Man, I conjured up all kinds of notions of what was going to happen to me. Diphtheria, under the best of conditions, was a serious thing. And these were not the best of times. I was placed way back in the corner of the barracks and told not to mingle with the other patients. They didn't look all that healthy, either. I spread out my blanket, stuck my helmet under my head and went to sleep.

Sometime later, a couple of doctors came, motioning me outside to the sunlight for a closer look. Each studied my throat again. One reached in his pocket and took a little pill about three-quarters of an inch in diameter and as thick as a dime, told me take it and drink lots of water. Like the old boy who was told to take two aspirin, go to bed and call him in the morning.

I had been coughing a lot with the sore throat and even after a good nights' sleep, I woke up to a spasm of coughing. That is, I slept as good as can be expected, sleeping with bamboo slats biting into my flesh. I felt something floating around in my mouth. I spit it out on my mess kit lid and out popped a thin white disk about 3/8th of an inch in diameter. I wrapped it in a piece of tissue paper that was handed out for toilet paper, to give to the doctor when I saw him later. He took one look at it and then at my throat and smiled, telling me it was not diphtheria and to keep drinking lots of water. He explained it was some type of yeast infection. The pill he had given me was nicotinic acid. If there were no more growth, he would send me back to duty side. Boy, was that a relief. I had already pictured myself bouncing along on one of those litters on the way to the bone yard.

Two days later, I was back on the work side. The sergeant had replaced me on the Japanese kitchen detail. Even as good as the food was over there, I was glad to be released from that detail. Those four days in the hospital, with all the rest and sleep, had repaired my wrestle worn muscles. It felt good not to hurt. So I returned to the farm detail and its daily monotony of carrying water, chopping weeds, picking veggies or working on a new project the Jap had thought up

They had the harebrained idea that they could cut a ditch through the levee that separated the river from the farm, which meant that at the highest point of the levee, the ditch had to be at least 15 feet deep. All went well on the first part, where the digging was not so deep. In that sandy loam, you just knew there would be cave-ins as the ditch got deeper. There were a couple of mishaps before I left for Japan in September, but after the surrender, I ran into some of the men who stayed at Cabanatuan, and they told me there was one cave-in that took several lives before the men could be dug out Like I have said, we were just numbers to the Jap

The encampment in Cabanatuan was surrounded by barbed wire fence with a guard tower spotted every 150 or so feet apart. Some enterprising prisoners in the barracks near the front that ran along the main road discovered a washed out place in the weeds and were slipping out and buying foodstuff and bringing it back to camp. The Jap guards caught six of them one night as they were coming back in, beat them severely, securely tied each one to one of the posts on which the barbed wire was strung, and left them there for two days and nights without food or water. At the same time, a detail was digging six slit trenches outside the fence, the width and length of a body. On the morning of the third day, each one of the six men was forced to stand at the foot of each trench. All prisoners were forced to line up along the fence while a Japanese firing squad assembled and fired one volley. As the men fell, they were supposed to fall in the ditch, but instead most fell half across the ditch. The officer in charge of the executions then methodically placed a pistol at the side of each POW's and fired, then brutally kicked the still threshing bodies into the ditch, after which he dismissed the firing squad and ordered the men who'd dug the ditch and were forced to watch, to refill the graves. The guard watched all the time until the job was completed. The prisoners were then dismissed and returned to the barracks to prepare for their respective details.

A few days later, orders came down from Japanese Imperial Headquarters that all prisoners would be divided into squads of 10 each, to be known as "buddy squads." If any one or more of that squad escaped, the others would be shot. This put everyone on good behavior. Just before we left for Japan, there was a rumor that someone had escaped. The Japanese sent out a squad to look for him and late that afternoon they came back, singing and marching in with the head of the man lashed to a pole. The next morning, nine prisoners with their hands tied behind them, were loaded on a truck and according the Japanese "honcho" (boss), were taken out and shot. After returning to the states, I was told that the man whose head was supposed to have been severed was later seen on the troopship coming back to the United States, along with some of the men in that death squad. If this was true, then whose head was on that pole? Who Knows? Probably some innocent Filipino.

The tone of our everyday conversation turned from 'wine, women and song' to that of food a good month before we were forced to surrender. From then on until I returned to the good old

USA, food was the uppermost thing in my mind. Food held the key to everything that existed. If you had food you had a better chance of staying healthy and being able to perform the many arduous tasks the Jap found. If they couldn't find one, they invented one.

It has been said by so-called authorities and philosophers, that sex is the great motivator, and I will agree, so long as the belly is full. But once the hunger pangs take over the body, sex goes out the door. As food took over being the great motivator; talks of chow, mostly in the past tense, was the main topic of the day. A lot of men even went so far as to think up fantasy recipes with all the ingredients in their proper portions laid out. I would like to have tried some of them after I got out of the service, but by then, the old mind had put food on the back burner and moved thoughts of 'cigarettes, whiskey and wild, wild women' to the front again. Nevertheless, in our starved state of mind and body, these recipes sounded good and helped pass the time until our next mess kit of rice and canteen cup of greens soup. Occasionally, other vegetables were thrown in, but not enough to really make much difference until the farm started producing a different bill of fare. Still, the diet lacked one main ingredient: protein.

On one occasion, the Japanese hauled in a couple of loads of coconuts, which had rotted on the ground. Eating ripe coconuts is a lot like taking a dose of Epson salts. Only worse. A couple of experiences with diarrhea caused by these coconuts was enough. The Filipinos eat the coconuts and drink the milk before it ripens and suffer no ill effects. Whether it was the oil or the fact that basically it is it a good source of fiber -something caused the diarrhea. I'm not an authority, so I won't venture an explanation. I know I only needed one time to learn my lesson.

The only use we found that we could enjoy from the coconuts wasn't exactly in a food form, but a beverage. Some of the men would ream out an eye in the coconut and pour sugar in the liquid then cork it back up to ferment. The inside meat and all made a fairly potent beverage. I don't know of anyone getting too inebriated on this liquid, but it was not uncommon to be wakened at night by one or two of these corked coconuts blowing out the cork with a loud bang. It did furnish some divertissement for the men.

I reflect back now on some of the things that went on in the prison camp and am amazed that any of us survived. I've heard people remark that they wonder how we made it. To be truthful, I keep asking myself the same question. We were stripped of just about every human dignity we ever possessed. It is a wonder we didn't kill each other off and save the Jap the trouble. But in each and every one of us there must have remained that one faint glimmer of hope and faith that we would endure. How else to explain the day in and day out frugal existence to which we had been reduced, without going stark raving mad.

Sure, the Jap were hard, brutal and sadistic, partly because of their culture, but partly because they were trying in the worst way to reduce us to the level of starving animals - fighting, snarling and scrapping over the smallest morsel of food, clothing or any other creature comfort. I believe we only got an inkling of the type of debauchery later honed to such a fine point on the American captives in Viet Nam. It all boils down to the intense hatred all the world holds for the United States.

I admit they succeeded to some extent. Yes, they humbled us. They stomped on us, beat us, starved us, but most of us kept coming back. Why? It was that indomitable spirit born of a free people, pulling themselves up by the bootstraps in the founding this great nation. We stood a head taller than the tallest Jap, and we knew it. In more ways than one. Granted, we left many good men over there, but they fought the good fight. We all have our breaking point. The Grand Architect of the Universe knows that better than anyone.

Most all the illnesses we had were a direct result of our starvation diet. Had we received adequate food, the body could have fought off the ravages of diseases such as diarrhea, Pellagra, wet and dry beri-beri, elephantiasis and numerous other frailties. Malaria and dysentery, which we all would have contacted sooner or later, would not have been so deadly had a proper diet been maintained.

A few limes, or more fresh vegetables would have lowered the cases of pellagra. Unpolished rice would have partially taken care of the beri-beri situation. Better sanitation facilities would have prevented many deaths. To say food, or rather lack of it, was the main cause of the high death rate is putting it mildly, as was clearly indicated when the Red Cross food was added to the inadequate rations being foisted on the camp.

Dry Beri-beri has a strange affect on the body. Caused by a lack of vitamin B-1 and Thiamine in the diet and characterized by a severe nerve disorder, it seems to affect the feet more than other parts of the body. You feel as if you set your feet down, they'll really hurt; but when you actually put your feet down, they feel better so long as you are on them. Then at night you suffer - your feet hurting so bad, and even worse in the toes and ball of the foot. For relief, we filled our helmets with cold water and sat with our feet in them. Other times, we partnered up and sat opposite each other, rubbing the feet of our partner. It felt so good. Sometimes we woke up in the night to rub the feet of someone who was hurting. If a person did not know the situation, they might have thought we had a foot fetish or something.

Wet beri-beri manifested itself differently on different people, sometimes the end being a heart dysfunction, or edema, where the legs start swelling, getting bigger and bigger as the swelling moves higher and higher until it reaches the viscera and stops the heart from beating. A corpse might weigh s much as 200 to 250 pounds of nothing but fluid. This was by far the deadlier of the two types of beri-beri.

Elephantiasis is a disease characterized by the enlargement of the body, especially the legs and genitals, and by the hardening and ulceration of the surrounding skin. It is caused by a breakdown in the lymphatic system due to an infestation of filarial worms. It resembles wet beri-beri, in that the legs also swell...only in beri-beri, both legs swell. Often, in cases of elephantiasis, only one leg will be affected. I was very fortunate in that I only had the dry type of beri-beri. My buddy and I sat up a lot of nights rubbing each other's feet - occasionally dropping off to sleep then waking back up with burning feet.

The Chaplains at Cabanatuan had quite a chore. Most of them sick and inflicted with the same diseases, and as sick, as the men they were comforting. Yet they continued doing the best they could with what they had to work with. Usually, a different Chaplain answered the burial detail call each day. I certainly had a lot of respect for these men who walked the extra mile in their duty to God and man. They deserve a lot of credit for the thankless task they performed during their internment I became very close to a Catholic priest who was a good friend of my "washed-out priest" friend. The three of us had many discussions about the immortality of man and the reasons for man's suffering, trials and tribulations and about the many other unanswered question that came up every day we were imprisoned. Most of the time they were talking over my head, which was understandable as they both were Catholic and well versed in their faith. I often listened in awe as they discussed and, at times, argued about subjects new to my limited knowledge of their religion, but they always came back to the same conclusion: there is no answer until God wants you to have an answer.

In this same vein, I knew a man just a couple of years older than I, who was a deacon in the First Christian Church of Portales, New Mexico, our home town. He was Senior Patrol leader of the Scout troop to which I belonged. He had a brother about a year younger. After I was drafted and sent to the 200th CAC and assigned to Battery H, I never saw any of the boys from my hometown except two or three times when we shared rides home on weekends. After imprisonment, we tried to keep in touch. . It was during one of these 'chance meetings' after arriving at Cabantuan, that I ran into him A surprise, as neither of us knew the other was in the Philippines. It really is a small world.

Anyway, he was in one barracks and I was in another. The way the Jap operated, you went to work by barracks, worked by barracks and marched back in by barracks, so I never saw him often until I came back from my diphtheria hospital stay, when I was assigned to the same barracks with him. I then learned he was having malaria attacks. They would come and go. He'd go out to work and get hot and that night he would have an attack. The two fellows who slept on each side of him were trying to take care of him, but one rainy night while making a latrine call, I noticed three figures under the eaves of the barracks, two supporting the third. When I was close enough, I saw the third figure was my friend from Portales, New Mexico. He was having a malaria attack and these buddies were trying to get his fever down by cooling him in the rainwater running from the roof. He was delirious, moaning, mumbling and threshing about so furiously it was hard to control him. I offered to help, and after 15 or 20 minutes, I would guess, he quieted down and they took him back to the barracks, dried him off, covered him and went back to bed. The next morning he was dead.

He was from a very close-knit family and I racked my brain to think of some way to let them know. So far, we had only been allowed to send a form card home with a few extra bits that was probably censored. Later, I got a letter from my mother telling me that my friend's father had died of a coronary. I thought, 'what a blow for that lady.' I knew the other sons had gone into the Air Corps before I was drafted.

A month or two after we arrived in Japan and were settled, the Jap let us write a letter home. This time we were able to write a short note at the bottom of the card. I wanted to tell this lady her son had died, but I didn't know how to word it so the Jap would not censor it. If I said he was dead, they were sure to black it out. So, knowing his father was recently deceased, I just wrote that my friend had joined his father. It went through. Later, I learned that this lady also got a call from the Air Corps that her other son had been shot down in Germany. She lost everything she had to WWII.

Sometime during the summer of 1943, a group of medics, some navy corpsmen and others came into possession of some musical instruments. At night after the evening meal, they got together in their barracks and started banging out a little jazz and popular tunes. It may not have been world class, but to our music-starved ears, it sounded like strains from heaven. As more instruments were acquired, they developed into a first class swing band. Some of the more accomplished musicians started putting the music down on paper for those musicians who couldn't play by ear could now join in. This was the beginning of out summer musicals, as we called them.

With the consent of the Japanese, who incidentally, liked the music as much as we did, a rough stage was built and music graduated into skits and finally plays - with the most outrageous costumes and uniforms you could have imagined. Thursday night musicals became so popular we had to set aside an area reserved for the Japanese to sit and watch. It is a wonder the actors didn't get chastised for some of the acts they performed, as most of the humor was jabs made at the Japanese in the form of satire. Whether they understood what was said and going on or not, they seemed to enjoy it as much, if not more, than we did. Before I left the camp to go to Japan, movies were even being shown. Of course, a lot of them were Japanese propaganda for the Greater East Asia Co-Prosperity Sphere. In a scene in one of the movies they showed the happy Filipinos mingling with the benevolent Japanese in a nightclub in Manila. The band was playing "Maria Elena," one of my favorite tunes of all time. I can't hear the tune without being taken back to that night so long ago, in the depressing and dehumanizing conditions that was Cabanatuan, without realizing how really, really lucky and fortunate I am to be here today. So many, many good men did not live to write about it.

I guess one of the most amusing incidents I recall happened while I was in the hospital for my suspected diphtheria. After I was cleared, I was moved to another barracks of men who were so thin...all skin and bones. They were the lucky few who were in the process of recuperating from a near-death experience. The hospital was divided into wards according to their condition, 0 to 5, zero being the death ward and 5 being men about to be sent back to the duty side.

I was in this #5 area where all were ambulatory and could get their food and feed themselves. There was probably not one man in that ward who weighed over 115 pounds. We had just returned from getting our evening meal when I heard this ruckus on the other side of the barracks. We all hurried around to see what was going on and came upon a sight that would boggle the eyes - these two 6 ft skeletons swinging their arms wildly about, trying to knock the other into the next county. At that time, it was hilarious. Every movement seemed to be in slow motion. I think they were only hitting fists and arms, and to top it off, all these other skeletons were hopping up and down screaming epithets and encouraging them. No one was trying to break it. I guess, because there was not much to break up. Before long, two corpsmen from the nearby barracks stepped in between them, sat them down and shoved their mess kits in their laps, telling them to eat. Then they turned to the rest of us and told us to eat. That was the end of it. Later in the evening, these two would-be pugilists were deeply engrossed in a game of chess with a homemade chess set. All this happened just after we had received the Red Cross boxes. I accepted and appreciated this, like most movie dramas, as comic relief after a very dramatic moment.

By the time we had been in prison camp six months, our well-worn shoes were worn out and discarded. At Cabanatuan, unless you were called up for one of the outside details like the wood cutters, you went barefooted or used some makeshift foot ware if you were lucky enough to find something to make do as a shoe. As a result of the so-called old 'Yankee ingenuity,' many styles of foot-ware emerged from a vast assortment of things available to keep the feet off the ground. The men on wood detail were issued a sort of high-top tennis shoe type foot-ware called a 'Tabi.'

Ever so often, the woodcutters would bring a chunk of balsa wood, which, when freshly chopped, is made up of about 80 percent water. As it dries and the water evaporates, it leaves a lightweight porous balsa wood. Many styles of sandals were from these one-time logs. Other woods were used, but were much harder to shape with the makeshift instruments used for that purpose. Finding strap material for these shoes was also a problem.

Other foot protectors were fashioned from the leather tops of worn-out and discarded shoes. A small piece could be cut and tied by a cord to the middle toe, allowing the leather to flop back under the ball of the foot, saving a lot of wear and tear on the heel. Cloth, canvas, burlap, even coconut husk served as foot protectors. Me? I went barefoot. When I was a kid, I could hardly wait until school was out to get my shoes off. By the time summer was over and school started again it was sheer torture to confine those rough and calloused feet back in those shoes again. After most of the stubble left when cogon grass was cleared off the farm, the sandy loam was not at all bad on the feet. Then, when they started laying out the rice paddies, shoes would have been out of place anyway.

We learned from a Jap we called 'Paddle foot,' to use the feet to form and pat the mud into the embankment to hold the water in. This nip had the biggest feet I have ever seen on a man. In some ways they really resembled paddles. He also knew how to use them to best advantage. You knew, when you saw him at work, these were not the first paddies he had built. We came to the conclusion that he was just an old Japanese farm boy, conscripted by their army. He was easy to work with and worked as hard as we did. He could also be hard-nosed if he thought you were trying to goof-off. So, going barefoot was nothing new to me and I made the best of it, thereby keeping the Jap off my back. It was amusing and even educational to see just how innovative and American one can be when one has to.

Like any large group of people confined to a small area, sanitation is the biggest problem, and Cabanatuan was no exception. We had all the same condition as at O'Donnell, but managed to profit from the many mistakes made there. Latrines were immediately dug and A-frame placed over them. Slack lime was found somewhere and used daily. As soon as a latrine filled up, it was covered and a new one dug. Bed bugs and lice were kept to a minimum with periodic delousing and debugging carried out. All bedding and clothing was steamed in boiling water to destroy eggs, nits and full-grown bugs and lice. Boiling water was poured on the bamboo slats where they were nailed to the floor joist. Mess kits and canteen cups were washed after each meal and dipped in boiling water to control bacteria. Everything that possibly could be done to make this camp reasonably disease free was instituted. Since the Jap were living in the same area, drinking and cooking with the same water, it was to their advantage these measure be taken.

When we arrived at Cabanatuan, the first detail I was placed on was improving the drainage problems. Hundreds of men spent days, almost a month, digging with pick and shovel so that the whole area would drain into the ditches running along the side of the highway that ran in front of the camp. The camp was situated high enough that drainage was not all that troublesome to correct, but using primitive methods to do it required a long time. But when it was completed we did not have any water standing to breed mosquitoes and flood the latrines.

During the rainy season, the A-frames over the latrines did pose a problem for the more infirmed men, especially those suffering from diarrhea and dysentery. The wet ground became quite slick during a rainfall and even the best of us had to watch our footing when using the A-frame. An incident I am not likely to forget happened one night while I was on guard duty. It had been raining steadily for some 24 hours or more, and when the Jap sounded their equivalent of 'Taps' or lights out, I took up my position sitting just inside to stay out of the rain. Guards were stationed at both ends of the barracks to make sure that anyone who leaves also comes back. We were on two hours shifts changing shifts when the Jap in the tower changed.

Not long after everyone was down and all was quite, one man with a bad case of diarrhea checked out to the latrine. I waited a reasonable time for him to return, then walked to the back of the barracks to see if he might have come in, but he hadn't. We then stepped out to try and see him, but the latrine was a good 50 feet from the barracks and in the rain nothing much could be seen. I thought I heard a faint sort of whine and the other guard heard it, too. The first thing that popped into my mind was that he had fallen in the trench under the A-frame. I took off, motioning the other guard to get some help if I needed it. Sure enough, when I got there he was up to his shoulders in the contents of that latrine, hanging on to one leg of the A-frame. I knew I could not get him out by myself, and about that time three other guys rushed up, moved the A-frame aside, grabbed him by both arms and lifted him out of that smelly hole. It was a good thing it was raining and running off the roof or we never would have cleaned him off just by throwing water from the spigot on him. I went back to my guard duty while the other three stood him under the eaves and washed him down. Just before I went off my shift, he pops up again. This time I escorted him down and back.

Rumors and rumors of rumors were the thing that kept us on our toes. It may have been a form of gossip. We knew some rumors had very little creditability. Maybe some malicious mind started these rumors just to see how far they would go. A work detail did not go out of camp without bringing back a bunch of unfounded rumors. One smart bird once remarked that we lived and breathed by the rumors. He was pretty close to being right.

Such was the big rumor that circulated around for almost a month, or until the time came and nothing happened. Peru, a neutral country, was going to intern all POWs until the outcome of the war was decided. We would be fed by the United States and given the same treatment as if we were in the service, but we could not be released until the war was over. A date had been set for our move. The Jap guards even heard this rumor and like us, waited for the day of departure. But the day came and went and we were still in the same place, doing the same things we had been doing for months, with the Jap guards having a laugh at our expense. Such was the tale of rumors. I guess it gave some the hope necessary to hang on a little longer. I can see how it might have worked the other way, either. Having ones hopes raised and then deflated so many times could make one want to give up, but I am not aware of any such cases.

We did, from time to time, get some news of what was going on from outside sources. This usually came from Filipinos who had access to short wave radios and managed to smuggle bits of news into the camp. Work details coming in from various parts of the island often had access to radio news and short wave broadcasts from Australia and San Francisco and brought the news when they were returned to the POW camp, but by and large we were pretty well cut off from the rest of civilization. Our little world revolved around the everyday humdrum existence that we maintained to keep half sane. As much as we hated the work we were forced to do, it was a lifesaver. I'd hate to think of having to pass all those many days I spent imprisoned and not having something to do or look forward to doing. . If not for any other reason, the work kept us constantly despising the Jap for their treachery, cunning and brutality and gave us something to live for and overcome each day. To me, it was as if they were daring us to survive, making each day a new challenge. Reflecting back on it now, it was just one day at a time, until?

Along about the middle of August 1943, we started hearing rumors of approaching Allied forces, and that the Jap were going to start evacuating all the POWs to Japan, Taiwan and Manchuria. Just how much truth there was of the Allied forces in the Pacific at the time, we were not sure. So we just put it down to idle rumors like all the rest. But when the Jap handed the barrack commanders a list of men to be given physical examinations, those rumors started to taking on some telltale sign of truth. I was on the list and as a U.S. and Japanese doctor both examined me, my name was put on another list along with 799 others. We were issued clothes including shorts instead of g-strings. The g-string heretofore had been our only bit of clothing, now we had a shirt, pants, socks, shoes and a cap to complete the boudoir. The next morning, all dressed up in our new clothes, we boarded trucks and pulled out of, never to see again, Cabanatuan Prison of War Camp #3. Where were we going now? Who knows!

I Was There, Charley

Aerial View of Hirohata POW Camp

CHAPTER FIVE
HIROHATA, JAPAN SEPTEMBER 3, 1943-- JUNE 19, 1945

It was September 3, 1943 when the Japanese delivered the paper listing the 800 men who were to be shipped out in the very near future. We left behind our old wardrobe, which consisted of a white cloth probably 30 to 36 inches long and 12 to 14 inches wide with a cord-like piece of cloth sewn across the narrow end of the cloth, simple and easy to put on. The string wrapped around the waist and tied in a bowknot with the cloth part hanging down in back, the loose end brought up between the legs and tucked under the string in front, and the remainder of the loose end hanging down. The Japanese military personnel wore these for underwear, and this was what we wore for outerwear. It was all we had. So we not only got 'a' change of clothes, we got 'some' clothes.

We hung around camp until the morning of September 18, 1943, resting and waiting for the inevitable. Rumors were flying like mad. Every time an officer came back from Japanese Headquarters, new rumors started. I think most of us pretty well knew where we were going by their picking the healthiest and most able-bodied, we were going where we'd have to work and work hard. With the Jap, that could be most anywhere. We only knew we were going to work as long as they had anything to do with it.

Not long after we had eaten the morning meal and the garden, wood choppers and gravediggers had gone to work; we were ordered to assemble in front of the Japanese headquarters where a string of trucks were lined up. We loaded up according to the usual fashion, like sardines, and were off to parts unknown. After leaving Cabanatuan City and heading down the main road we all were so familiar with and along which so many lives had been lost, it was a pretty good sign our destination was Manila. Arriving in the afternoon, we proceeded straight to Pier 7 where we boarded the

I Was There, Charley

"Nissyo Maru," a light two-hole freighter, with four hundred men in the front hole, and another four hundred in the aft hole. Here we sweated out the next two days in that hot, humid, stinking hole with next to no fresh air circulating. On the morning of the third day, we felt the vibration of the propellers as the ship began to move out of the harbor. A short time later, the hatch was partially opened and we inhaled the first breath of fresh air in three days. We were on our way.

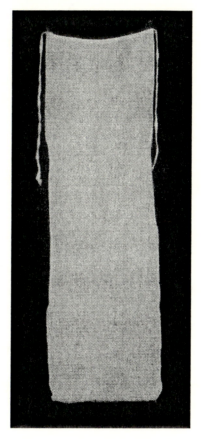

Japanese underwear

The next seven days were pretty humdrum. The China Sea during the fall of the year can spawn some of the worst storms in that part of the globe. The space allotment for each man was, at most, 24 inches wide and maybe 7 ft in length. The hole was double decked and the only way out was up a steel ladder through a small opening in the hatch cover at the top. No one was allowed on deck except to go to the toilet - a two-holer suspended half off the deck over the water below. During most of the journey the weather was wet and the wind blew hard. A rope was strung from the exit hole to the toilet to keep us from being blown overboard, just like on our other trip - and like I said before, no one made that trip unless they were in dire need.

Food and water was lowered on a rope in a bucket and dipped up into the mess kits and canteen cups twice a day. Maybe the Jap figured if we were not working, we wouldn't need much food, and it was adequate. The first few days a lot of the men were so sea sick they couldn't eat what they were served. We never removed our clothing, the whole trip from the Philippines to Japan. The rice straw mats were so rough and the motion of the ship such that most of us soon developed blisters and/or raw spots. As a result, a lot of sleeping was done in an upright position. The days were long and the nights longer, with little chance to determine whether it was day or night (unless we made a trip to the toilet). Lights were kept on during the daylight hours in the hole, but turned off at night. The leg from Manila to Takao, Taiwan, was from dullsville, with us trying to think of some way to pass the time. Then another rumor, this one that a submarine alert had gone out, and the hatch door was bolted shut. The weather was so bad I doubt a self-respecting submarine would have been in those waters. On the morning of September 25, 1943 we put in at Takao, Formosa, now known as Taipei, Taiwan. Three days were spent there loading on more food for the final run to Japan. We were allowed to come on deck and watch the sampans in the harbor and the oarsmen rowing small boats loaded with supplies for the freighter. This went on day and I guess, night. We were run back in the hole for the evening meal and kept there through the night. The harbor was very picturesque, in spite of the conditions under which we had to view it. You would never know there was a war going on by looking at it as we were. The harbor is almost completely surrounded by a mountain range with only a small passageway on one side to allow ships to come and go. It was so quiet and peaceful, we felt like we were leaving some revered place.

Once we had cleared the breakwater and headed out to sea, the peace and quiet gave way to the violence of the wind and rain, experiencing again what we'd gone through for the past six or seven days before entering the harbor at Takao. For the next seven days it was more of the same…all the way to Moji harbor on the southern tip of the island of Honshu. Arriving in the late afternoon of October 5, 1943, we were put ashore and marched to a railway station nearby, where we had our first experience with unisex rest rooms. It was somewhat embarrassing, but we lived over it. As the sun set behind the mountain range surrounding the port of Moji, the fall breeze wafted across the station platform and soon penetrated our tropic wear. We were forced to huddle up close to keep warm as we sat and waited for the train that was to take us to our destination. After almost becoming icicles, a train finally backed in and we gladly boarded it. It may not have been all that cold, it was just that we were only fifteen days out of the tropics and hadn't adjusted to the change in climate. The four hundred men in the fore hole evidently traveled in another direction, as I never saw or heard of them again.

We rode the train all night and most of the next day, getting very little sleep in those small coaches with small seats that had to accommodate two Americans, but built for the Japanese. Oh, I think I dropped off a few times, but not for long. It seemed they liked to start and stop a lot. The next morning the train stopped at a small place and "binto" bo xes were brought aboard for all of us. It was filled with rice, some sort of fish, daikon and a vegetable. Not all that much but filling, especially since we had not had anything to eat in over 24 hours. Wooden buckets of water were brought aboard, enabling us to fill our canteens. Restroom facilities were small rooms in the end of the cars with little more than a slit in the floor. The trip reminded me of the old milk trains running here in the States. I didn't know if it was a regular train or a special one just for the purpose of carrying POWs. The people at each station were just as curious about us as we were of them, but we were not allowed to open the windows to even try to make conservation with them, so we just stared at each other. The ride was rather a picturesque one along the coastline. Small towns and villages dotted the hillside along the way, with terraced rice paddies on the side of the mountains. We received one more "binto" similar to the one we had received in the morning, so we assumed it was a noon meal. We arrived at the Hemiji station late in the afternoon and by the time we had detrained, lined up and marched the short distance to the camp at Hirohata, it was getting dark.

We marched to the camp, lined up again and counted off. The men whose numbers were from 1 to 160 were told to occupy the barracks immediately behind us. The remainder would occupy the one in the back part of the camp running parallel with the back fence. I was number 148, so I was assigned to the front barracks. There were 400 men in the group, so we wondered why the inequity in the number assigned to each barracks. Then men dressed in sailor suits directed us to various parts of the barracks until both the lower and upper berths were filled. Eighty-four men, navy and marines captured on Guam, were already occupying these barracks and wore numbered tags from 1 through 84, thus explaining the inequity.

The barracks resembled a large warehouse type building with windows all around the side and ends. Two rows, double tiered, with bunks head to head, ran the full length of the building allowing only enough room at the end and on the sides to accommodate a shelf, 1-foot wide, to serve as an eating space and ten-foot benches to sit on plus room for passing. A wide passageway ran down the middle with a large table and benches used for eating and walking. In the center of the barracks stood a large coke or wood stove to knock off the chill in the winter, which is just about all it did, it sure didn't give off much heat. We thought the men in the upper deck fared better, since heat rises, but they insisted it didn't make all the much difference. There was an entrance on one side of the barracks, which was the only way in or out, making it easy for them to guard, but would have proven deadly had there been a fire. The windows were too little to allow an escape, as the Jap found that out later when the United States started dropping incendiary bombs and hit a

POW barracks in the Kobe harbor area. I was through Osaka on the way to a new camp in early 1945 when I met a bunch of those men who were burned in that blaze. They were a pretty horrible looking group, and they were the lucky ones, as they said. Many died in that fire.

This was a brand new camp. They were still finishing up some of the facilities when we arrived. The men from Guam had been there some time and had even aided in the construction. The camp was enclosed within a solid 12-foot wall completely encircling it. Besides the two large barracks, there was the Japanese headquarters with living areas in one end. One building housing the Navy Corpsmen and Doctor and sick call room, a small hospital enclosure, .two long wash racks, food storage rooms, and large 4-kawa kitchen, shower and bathing facilities. Two toilet areas made up the compound. A large assembly area was in the middle of the camp, opening to the outside through a large heavy double gate big enough to allow a truck to enter and was used for the coming and going of the work force every morning and evening. All the buildings were of wood construction, built on concrete slabs and covered with concrete tiles. Serviceable and new was about all I could say about it, but it was a far, far cry from the quarters in the Philippines.

After we all were petty well settled in, the Guam people brought in several buckets of rice and thin vegetable soup which they doled out, telling us to enjoy because that was the last time they would be doing it. A U.S. Marine First Sergeant then came in and divided us into groups of 60 men each and asked if anyone in each group was a sergeant. Two or three of us held up our hands. I was picked from my group and was put temporarily in charge. As soon as all the groups were formed, we were told we were to have a meeting later on that night. My promotion to Sergeant had been infield, and therefore could not be recognized, so I was put back to Corporal. But not before I made out like a Sergeant for a couple of days. Actually, the only thing I did was appoint a mess crew that went to the kitchen each meal to pick up the food and dish it out and call the men to attention when a Jap came through the building or when we had head-count at night. I was in charge of squad three and it had sixty men in it. When I called for "count off," I was number one and the last man had better be 60. After the first night, the Jap guard told us that count off would be in Japanese.

I had learned how to count in Japanese while I was working in the Japanese kitchen in Cabanatuan. If you can count from one to ten, you have it made. 1 is Itchi, 2 is Ni, 3 is San, 4 is Sche, 5 is Go, 6 is Roku, 7 is Sieche, 8 is Hotchi, 9 is Cue, and 10 is Ju.(the spelling may not be exact, but you can get the idea. 11 would 10 and 1 or ju-itchi. 12 would be 10 and 2, or ju-ni. 20 would be 2+10 or ni-ju. 21 would be 2+10+1 or ni-ju-itchi. And so on. When you get to 100, that is haiku. So 131 would be 100+3+10+1 or haiku-san-ju-itchi. 200 would be 2+100 or ni-haiku. 251 would be 2+100+5+10+1 or ni-haiku-go-ju-itchi.

You can imagine trying to teach this over a 24-hour period. We squad leaders got together and assigned each man a number and made sure he got in the right position so when he said a number in Japanese we had taught him to say he would be in the right place to say it. We had a few practice sessions and gave each man a slip of paper with his number on it. It wasn't perfect by any means, but I think the Jap guard was impressed enough that he didn't "batsu" (hit) any one over it. You really never knew if you ever satisfied them or not

Outside of learning to count in Japanese, the first three days were spent in filing out forms that were given to us in both languages. It was the usual, name, rank and serial number, which is all you are to give according to the Geneva Convention. But the Japanese did not recognize the Geneva Convention, except when it was convenient for them, so we also filled out our date of birth, occupation, education, country, state, town, and a few other trivialities. The Marine First Sergeant said they were looking for technicians and college educated personnel to be used in the war effort. He advised us to not help them any more that we had to, so we didn't.

By the end of the third day, I had lost my job (which did not make me mad), but the whole group of men were numbered starting with number 85, the highest ranking non-com in the new group getting that number, then the next highest rated non-com 86 and so on though the ranks down to the lowest private getting the largest number. I had been demoted to a Corporal because field promotions might not be recognized in the U. S. Most field promotions on Bataan never reached the War Department, so I was a Corporal and any report other than that would confuse those in Headquarters and delay action, which, in some cases, could be serious. So I ended up with #208-ni-haiku-hotchi. I was moved to another squad, but stayed in the same building. We were all issued our number tags with very strict orders to wear them at all times. Later on we were issued heavy coats for the upcoming winter, and a stamp with interchangeable numbers so your number could be stamped above the pocket of your coat. You had to have your number on you somewhere or a guard might think you were swapping coats and making too many trips to the toilet.

On the fourth morning, the mess crews brought the food over for breakfast, and when we returned the bucket, they refilled it with another ration to put in our mess kits for the noon meal. Then it dawned on us…the vacation was over and we were on our way to work. The men from Guam had been going to work the three days we were getting organized. Today they would have company. Big company…four hundred more. At this time, I weighed 159 pounds.

The road to the Seitetsu Steel Mill ran down the side of the camp and was accessible from the big double gate on the side of the enclosure. It was about one mile away and took a little over twenty minutes to walk it. When we arrived at the gate of the mill, we were lined up to get the number needed for that particular day. If there was an ore boat in, the ore company honcho, in charge of unloading, would get the number of men needed and the day would be spent in the hole of the ship shoveling iron ore. If it was the coal company with a ship in port, the day was spent shoveling coal. These two companies usually took the majority of the men. Others might work the rolling mill where you shoveled chunks of metal broken off the red-hot slab as it passed through the rollers. You watched and got out of the way as the slab came by, or a hot piece of slag off the slab could go down your neck and give you a bad burn. Some men went to the naphthalene plant and shoveled flakes into stacks to be loaded later into rail cars. The foul smell from these hot flakes often resulted in bad headaches.

The first detail I caught was on the scrap-iron heap. When we arrived to work in this steel mill, there were long piles of scrap iron everywhere you looked. The Jap had stripped the island they occupied of all scrap metal, even going so far as to dismantle operating textile mills and breweries, and any and all types of manufacturing that had steel or iron in it. This was loaded onto ships and sent to the steel mills in Japan. Our job was to break these big hunks of metal into little hunks of metal so it could be fed into the smelters along with raw ores and white rock. Most of the metal was cast iron and easily broken with a 16-pound sledgehammer. If you couldn't break it with that, you struggled with a pneumatic jackhammer until it was pulverized. Any way you cut it, we were in for hard manual labor.

Another backbreaking job was on the slagheap. Slag is the residue that rises to the top of the molten metal when iron is being separated from the other ingredients. This was then drained off into railroad cars, carried to dumping grounds and used as landfill. After it solidified and cooled enough, the men who were not chosen for company details would be assigned to the slagheap and with a pick, they were put to work 'making little one out of big ones.' We were often sent out before the slag had cooled sufficiently, resulting in serious burns. In the winter, this could be a warm place to work, but in the summer it was doubly hot with the sun beating down. You just had to take the bitter with the better, but the better only happened once in a great while.

The few motor vehicles we saw around the mill were either powered by a liquid derived from the process of breaking down coal, or had a coke burner in back of the cab, that burned coke and used the gas generated to run them. Needless to say, this was the reason there were so few of them, and accounted for the way they sort of limped around. One did not have to be a whiz kid to see these trucks and diminishing scrap iron piles, to know that the Japs were hurting internally. In spite of the fact that the mill was supposed to be running at full blast, the quantity of sheet steel that was being turned out was nil when it comes to supporting a war effort. All we had to do was look around us and see there was no way they could carry on a prolonged war with this type of equipment and shortages with which they were working. They were using us as slave labor to offset the millions of men they were pressing into their various services. Their equipment was so antiquated that to this day I can't understand why they thought they could fight a successful war with the United States.

To be picked to work at unloading one of the ships, either coal or ores, was a chance to get extra chow. One could always sneak off on a toilet break, locate the ships galley and mooch some food or find the storeroom and slip something down your pants leg to sneak into camp. It was best you ate it on the ship because, if there was a shake down and you were caught with stolen goods, you not only got the shit beat out of you, the squad you were working with had to stand out in the courtyard all night and was still expected to work the next day, regardless of whether if was in the heat of summer or near freezing in the winter. No food for that night or the next morning. In spite of the penalties, there was a lot of food brought into camp. If I was even lucky enough to come into possession of some illegal food, I ate it on the spot. Every time I worked a coal or ore ship, I held my breath until we were checked in at night. I stood in the courtyard one night in November and it got right chilly before morning. The three guilty men, who were caught, were tied to a sort of an affair that resembled the old time hitching post in front of the local saloons, beaten with a wooden stick and left there all night. To make it more impressive, the Jap on guard periodically doused them with water. You would think some people would learn, but fools never do and thus live to make the same mistakes over and over.

There were four of us who had bunks in the same location, went to work together and most of the time got picked for the same detail at the mill. We later told the three that caused the penalty that if it happened again and we were on their detail, they had better give their hearts to God, because after the Jap got through with them their ass belonged to us. And we were not joking. I guess my luck held up because I never was subject to that penalty again.

The only time I came close to getting in trouble, we were working a coal ship freighter. It was close to quitting time and the ship was another hour or so from being unloaded. We figured we had to work until it was finished and sure enough, as we were getting ready to climb the ladder out of the hole, the head "hancho" started hollering, "No stop, No stop, Sanyo, Sanyo," so back to the coal mines we went. By this time we were having to shovel the coal out of the corners and along the sides half way to the spot where the bucket came down to pick it up, then another group would shovel it a second time to the middle of the floor. The Jap honchos must have been as pissed off as we were, because they were pushing twice as hard as usual. One little 'pip-squeak' had been riding me all day and I was about at my boiling point when he hit me one too many times with that stick and I drew my #4 coal scoop back, about to unload on him when my buddy grabbed the scoop. That is all they wanted, an excuse to use their sticks. Actually, they were not supposed to hit us, but report any infraction to the prison guards. They worked me over good, four or five of them, but I didn't yield. Finally, we all went back to work and finished the unloading.

When we got back to the mill gate, I was sure to get another working over by the Jap Camp guards. We counted off to make sure we were all there and then turned to the Jap guards and walked back to camp where we counted off again and were dismissed, drew our chow which was cold by now, went to the barracks and ate it. This was not our bath night, so a couple of my buddies went out to the wash rack with me. I removed my clothes to check for marks. I could feel most of them, but none showed if I had my clothes on. I had blue and green bruises for the next two weeks but never missed a day of work. Not one of the four of us ever got picked for the coal ship after that. It might have just been coincidental, but I don't think so.

I never worked an iron ore ship but once. Unloading coal is hard enough, but you a least can get the shovel into it. Working iron ore is just like trying to shovel large rocks glued in red clay.

It is about the hardest work I did all the time I was in prison camp. How we ever got that boat unloaded, I will never know. There was one bright spot, however; we were given a small ration of rice with some sort of boiled fish in it, after which the ships' cook set a basket of Japanese persimmons out for us. The only persimmon I ever ate. At the time, it seemed a rare delicacy.

Around Thanksgiving it was getting colder and the chow was not getting any better…we ate the same old thing, day in and day out: rice and thin greens soup. We just couldn't work like we were being forced to work on the kind of food we were being fed. I knew I was losing weight, and I could feel it in the way my clothes fit. Come Thanksgiving, we expected something a little different. Maybe better, but no! Thanksgiving is not one of their holidays, so every body works and the menu of the day is rice and greens soup.

December 17, 1943 was a tragic day for all of us. We knew there were several men in the hospital, but didn't realize some of them were as sick as they were. Cpl. Arthur A. Hall in our group of 60, died of pneumonia. Sgt. Clouse, our squad leader, appointed four of us to stay in camp, as per order of the Japanese, to take care of the burial. We went to the mill with a four-wheel cart drawn by two bulls to get a wooden barrel in which to put the body so it could be cremated. While we were there, some heavy timbers were loaded on the cart for the cremation. A Jap guard accompanied us. He and the driver rode as we walked Indian-style, two men on each side of the wagon. Bulls are not the speediest animals in the world, so it took us three hours to walk that mile, load the barrel and timbers and walk the mile back.

Then came the serious part - how to get the body in that wooden barrel. This man was probably 5-ft, 8-inches and, although thin on the starvation diet we were getting, could not have weighed over 120 or 125 pounds. The barrel is maybe 36-inches tall, maybe 24-inches at the top and bottom and bulging out to 30-inches around the middle. It had a bottom in it and a lid to cover it. We had picked the largest barrel we could find from a room full of barrels of all sizes. Finally the Japanese honcho from crematory (just down the road from the camp) arrived and proceeded to show us how to get the body in the barrel. Their custom is to return the body to the fetal position in the womb. This was not going to be an easy task, but the old maestro had evidently done this a good many times and had no trouble. He set the body upright, folded the knees under its chin, wrapped the arms around the shinbones and with the our help, lifted it up and dropped it in the barrel, slapped the top on and directed us to put it on he bull cart with the timbers. He then climbed aboard and off we went. We pulled up beside a giant oven-like affair with a firebox on the bottom and a tall chimney in the rear. He opened the big cast iron door and directed us to place the barrel on a steel plate that rested on the grate in the oven, then closed the door and proceeded to start a fire in the firebox. After getting the fire to burning quite briskly, he started piling on the larger timbers. When everything seemed to be going according to Hoyle, he said something to the Jap guard, who turned to us and pointed to the watch on his wrist. It was 12:30 p.m. He pointed to the figure 4 saying "we come," then motioned us to follow as he hopped bull cart and directed the driver back to the camp. When there, the bull cart went on its way and the guard directed us to wait outside the office. Shortly, Taharasan, (the 'san' at the end of a name denotes Mr.) the interpreter for the camp, came out and told us to go to the kitchen and get our skimpy meals and he would come for us a 4 p.m., at which time we would return to the crematory with the urn to retrieve the ashes of our departed countryman.

Actually, this had not been a half-bad day. We lay on our bunks until Tahara came for us. He walked ahead and we followed in twos with the guard bringing up the rear. The crematory honcho was still there. When he opened the door, Tahara handed us the urn and the honcho, using a scoop, placed scoops of ashes in the urn. Upon returning the urn to Tahara, we noted a tag glued to the side with some Japanese script engraved on it. He said it was an identification tag. He placed the top on the urn and we returned to camp in the same formation we left, then we were dismissed. Tahara and the guard went to the offices. It had been quite a day. I had one other such experience while I was on light detail not long before I changed camp.

In this case, I remember it so well because we could not find a barrel big enough to contain the body. The old honcho tried every trick he knew but the barrel just was not deep enough to accommodate the body of a 6-foot 6-inch man. A casket-like box was built at the mill and sent out the same day, as the body would not have lasted another 24 hours. We did not get the casket until after 3:00 p.m. and by the time the honcho got the body in the small box it was after 4:00 p.m. before the fire was built. When we finally got the urn filled and back in camp it was after 8:00 p.m. A long day.

Hirohatta POW Camp

At Hirohata, as I said, the camp was still being completed. We had been waiting for a bath for the 18 days on the boat and in route to Hirohata from Moji, as we all smelled and looked like hell. But, since Hirohata was not complete with a bath, we used the running water at the wash racks. With our canteen cups, we poured water over ourselves, lathered up and rinsed off in what I would estimate was a high of 50 or low of 60-degree temperature. Although cold, I would put that bath among the best I ever had. It wasn't until almost a month later our big communal hot tub was completed, and we could take cold showers and sit in a warm hot tub. That felt so fine after a cold day at the mill.

Two or three times, before the bath facilities were ready, we were taken to the Hirohata communal bathhouse. The Jap made arrangements for all the residents to be out when we arrived and they were not allowed back in until we left. It was probably a half-mile there and we went in our skivvy shorts or G-string. Shucks, we met Japanese civilians coming and going in even less. There were male and female sections but no partition between them. There was a concrete barrier between the two tubs. We were required to shower off with cold water and then enter the cooler portion of the tub and gradually become accustomed to the temperatures. We gradually moved closer to the heater located down one side of the tub, where the water was hottest. I could stand it pretty hot, but I never went all the way to the heater. Later on in the winter, when the days were shorter and it was getting dark by the time we got back to camp, on a cold day we would see the civilians coming out of those hot baths, their bodies fairly steaming in the cold air. In winter, the only time I could sleep all night without waking was on the nights we had hot baths, which was two nights a week. My body was so hot covers weren't needed until it cooled. On other nights, we had so little bedding I slept cold all night, not getting a good nights' sleep.

The majority of the men still kept their hair clipped for cleanliness. Unlike Cabanatuan, we were allowed razor blades. As a rule, we kept closely shaved even though a lot of us just used clippers on our head and face. After being forced to work a day in a coal ship, especially in summer months, in a slag heap rolling mill, you were covered from head to foot with grime of one sort of another so it just made good sense, if we were to keep clean, to clip it all off.

One guy in our barracks, Squad #6, flatly refused to bathe. The squad leader stayed on him all the time. As it got colder and colder, he kept putting off bathing longer and longer. His hair and beard got so long it was filthy with coal dust, dirt and grime of all kinds. The squad leader kept telling him if he did not straighten up and fly right he would go to the first sergeant. We knew the Jap might pull this guy out of line some day and penalize the whole barracks for his condition. So, about a dozen of the guys who had to sleep close and smell him, warned him that if he did not clean up, they would clean him up. He dared them to try it. Two afternoons later, on bath night, they caught him coming out of one of the toilets and hustled him off to the bathhouse, yelling and cussing. With bristle brush and issue soap, they scrubbed him from head to foot, then put him in the hot tub and held him there to soak, then dried him off and clipped his hair and beard. They had him clean for once. The next afternoon he came in and made sick call. He was running fever and was supposed to have had pneumonia. The medics kept him in the sickbay for a couple of days, then returned him to duty. But he did not reform. He remained the same slob, still having to be threatened to clean up.

The one thing that was not tolerated in POW camps was stealing. Few of us had anything of real monetary value, but what we did have, had sentimental value. If there ever had been anything worth keeping, the Jap long ago had it. The only 'valuables' I possessed were a couple of notebooks that served as address books and tidbits of information I picked up from time to time, a stub pencil that had just about written its last words, a 20 reales piece (Spanish silver coin of the early 1800s about the size of a silver dollar) that I had so far been able to hide from the Jap, my bedding, clothes, mess kit, canteen and canteen cup. I found the coin while digging a grave at O'Donnell. No telling how long it had been buried there. As a collector's item, it is not all that valuable. But I still keep it anyhow.

In spite of the intolerance of stealing, it went on. Most of it involved food items. This was especially frequent during the period we received Red Cross packages. A man might leave some article wrapped up in his bedroll. Each morning your bedding had to be rolled up and positioned at the head of the bunk space and most of us rolled all our belongings in the bedroll. When we came in from work, we unwrapped our bedroll and if something was missing, the first thing was to suspect a bunkmate or men in your vicinity who might know what you'd put in the bedroll. The Jap took a dim view of stealing also, and they would call everyone out and have an overall shake down, so we were leery of reporting a thief to them. As a result, a lot of people got blamed for thieving and most of them may have been innocent Consequently, there was a lot of hard feelings and tension in the barracks. As if we did not have enough problems.

The 1st Sergeant decided to take action on his own and take care of any reported theft himself. He held his own shakedown, unknown to the Jap and dished out his own brand of punishment. This must have got the offenders attention, for stealing slowed a lot. Then after one case where the thief received 10 lashes with a Sam Brown belt across the naked back, it ceased or was not reported at all. I think if I had had to be punished for an infraction against my fellow POW (perish the thought) I would rather have it at the hand of one of my own than by the Jap.

Christmas 1943 came and went, just another day of the many miserable days that ran together into weeks and weeks of back breaking work and starvation. Men were falling out right and left on the job, to be ruthlessly prodded back to work to fall out again. The hospital in the camp was almost to capacity with men suffering from extreme cases of Beri-Beri, fatigue, fever and pneumonia. By the first of the year, three more men had died and 15 or 20 more were just hanging on. At that time I was down to 135 pounds.

We were all suffering various stages of Beri-Beri, pellagra, boils, Chinese rot, you name it and one of us had it. As in Cabanauan, there was little to treat these maladies. The mill had a hospital, but you had to be nearly dead to be sent there. The Japanese medic was a perverted navy medical corpsman who thought he was the answer to Doctor Switzer. He was well known for his weekly short arm inspections. With a long pair of forceps he would sit on his lazy ass and have the men, dead tired from a day at the mill, parade by and lower their trousers so he could look at, and with the forceps, squeeze their sex organs. I guess that was the way he got his jollies.

On January 25, 1944, the Japanese finally allowed a Red Cross package to be issued to each man. This was a lifesaver in more ways than one. First, it furnished something to augment the measly ration we were getting and secondly, it was a psychological kick in the butt to all the POWs. A week later the Japanese Army took over the feeding of the prisoners and a definite change was noted in the rations. I guess the three more deaths in January got their attention. Who knows? During this time I developed a large boil on the shin of my left leg. It was so swollen and painful, I could hardly walk. I was still limping to the mill and if I did not have to do much walking, could do enough to keep the Nip honchos off my butt. I was hoping it would come to a head so I could mash the core out, but such was not the case. Finally, I made sick call one afternoon. The navy corpsman took one look and lanced it, removed the core, put a stitch in it, dressed it and I went back to work the next morning. It felt so much better, I could have danced to work. The next day, on February 8, 1944, I got my first letter from home. It had been written over a year before. My girl friend from Lubbock had been to see my folks, my brother had been inducted, one sister was working and the other was getting ready to graduate from high school. I'd had no word from then since before Pearl Harbor, so this was all news even if it was over two years old. Evidently they had not received any of my short notes because they still were not sure of my status.

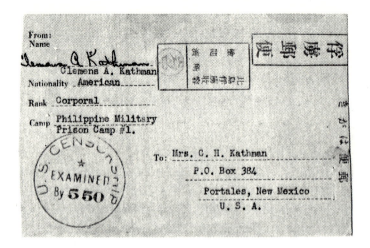

Post Card Home Side #1

Post Card Home Side #2

By February 20, during a rest day we were allotted every two weeks, we had a weigh-in and I was back up to 142. The increase in rations and the Red Cross packages had definitely helped. Men started to be a little more hopeful of the situation. There was definitely a more positive attitude. Some of the enthusiasm was probably due to the church services that were being allowed from Japanese ministers and a priest. These were few and far between, but were well attended by men of all faiths. I can safely say that I never met an atheist in that POW camp or any other POW camp. Although there were no chaplains or pastors to conduct funeral services, a prayer was always offered in behalf of the deceased.

The conditions under which we were forced, affected every man differently. Only an experienced psychologist or sociologist would even try to explain the whys and wherefores. At this time, all of us were to busy trying to stay alive and keep our sanity, but reflecting back over the years I can definitely see that each man dealt with problems in the best way he knew. For me, faith and hope were the big factors in survival. Never, in my mind, even when I was so far down, did it occur to me that I might not be going back home. It was not 'if' I get out of this mess, but 'when' I get out of this mess. A sort of one day at a time attitude until...

There were a few incidents of men who lost it. That is to say, they had a psychological change due to the conditions under which they were subjected. A couple of cases come to mind. The first was a big quiet lug of a guy from one of the north central states. He was easy going, never had much to say and was never argumentative. The last person you'd expect to do anything to bring the Jap wrath down on him. Gradually, we began to see and definite change in his mannerisms. He became openly belligerent to the men working around him, going so far as to openly defy the Japanese, which resulted in some severe beatings. At one moment he could be as nice a person as you would want to know and then something would be said or done and he would go berserk. If left alone, he was a happy, jovial soul. It finally got so bad the Japanese refused to send him out to work. He was left in camp to his own devises, talking to himself and doing his own thing. I left Hirohata a few months before Japan surrendered, so I never know what happened to him.

The other case was a rough and hard talking, hard drinking old boy from Kentucky who got religion. It was such an obsession with him that he got to be a nuisance to all those around him. He would be on the job and out of the blue he would start on this diatribe about the condition the world was in, opening the bible he carried with him at all times, as if to prove his point. Some of the men who knew him from way back said he could hardly read or write. These antics, as serious as they were to him, resulted in a lot of punishment for him and the squads in which he was working. Such was the way the Jap doled out punishment. The action of one man in a group reflected on the group as a whole and all received a modicum of blame. As the old fisherman told his fellow fisherman, "All fishermen are liars except me and you and sometimes I don't know abut you." The same could be said about all of us being crazy.

The surrounding country around the camp was rice paddies and vegetable garden, beautifully terraced and well tended. The first thing we noticed on our way to the mill was the buckets suspended on each end of a pole the Japanese farmers were carrying up and down the rows of vegetables. Upon further inquires, we found out these were fertilizer buckets. The rural Japanese use all types of fecal matter for fertilizer, including the human type. They came in the camp periodically and emptied out the huge concrete tanks beneath our benjzos (toilets) and sprinkled the contents on the ground around the vegetables. At least this was one chore we did not have to do. I just tried not to think about it while I was eating, especially when eating greens soup. Of course, if you are hungry you don't think. It's better that way.

Late in February 1944, I began having back pain I could not explain. It was not so bad in camp, but on the job where most of our work was shoveling and bending over, became excruciatingly painful at times. Thinking it could be my kidneys, I started making myself drink more water, hoping that might solve the problem. Unfortunately, the pain was still there and I began to note a lack of feeling and weakness in my right leg. Still I continued to work. When one of my buddies commented on my dragging right leg, I decided to check in with the medics. After I returned to camp and had a hot bath, I felt much better. The next morning, March 8, 1944, it was a different story. I could not even move my right leg. I had no use of it at all. My buddies told the squad leader, and after checking with me, reported it to the medics. Captain Seid, the doctor who had accompanied the group from the Philippines along with the Jap corpsman, came to my bunk to check on me. The Jap corpsman demanded that I get up. I managed to scoot to the end of the bunk and stand on my left leg, my right one just dangling. He kicked my right leg. It still hung limply and I didn't feel a thing except a dull thud when his boot struck the leg. He turned to the doctor and motioned that it was all his, turned and walked off. Two corpsmen who accompanied Captain Seid, one on each side, walked me to the dispensary. Captain Seid examined me and told them to put me in the hospital area. He didn't say, but one of the corpsmen said it was probably Beri-Beri.

Although Captain Seid continued to examine me, he was not sure what was causing the paralysis. After two weeks to 15 days, he noticed a knot or bulge in the right groin, the area where the most pain seemed to center. It was then that he began to think it might be appendicitis and moved me to the little hospital off the dispensary. I had been eating very little in spite of the improvement in the food ration. I hurt so bad I was sick at my stomach and did not feel like eating. By the time I was moved into the little hospital, I had dropped to 115 pounds. During this time, the Captain tried to get me in the Mill Hospital, but the Japanese Corpsman would have none of it. However, some of the doctors from the mill hospital came to see me, but nothing ever came of it. I think the Jap Corpsman thought I was faking. Hell, who knew what that pervert thought.

After the visit by the mill doctors and getting nothing done, Captain Seid decided to take care of the situation in the best way he knew how. After another near sleepless night, on the morning of April 17, 1944, Navy Corpsman Bob Epperson a Guam POW working in the dispensary, brought me two big blue pills called 'Blue Heavens' and had me take them. Blue was their color, heaven was where you felt like they took you. It took about thirty minutes for them to take effect, at which time Captain Seid and Epperson returned with a washbasin, gauze, his freshly sterilized straight razor and other medical paraphernalia. He thought he knew the problem and told me what he proposed to do about it. By this time, he could have cut off a leg and it would have been all right with me.

He turned me over, about halfway on my left side. After that I don't remember much except dull pressure along the area of right groin. I had no concept of time and it was only when I felt something warm trickling across my back toward the left side and I must have made some movement, when the Captain told me it was all over. Bob was flushing my insides out with a solution of potassium permanganate. He said I should be getting some feeling back in my leg in a day or two. After the corpsman finished, he put a bandage on the incision and turned me on my back again. Then he showed me the washbasin that was half full of a greenish white stuff, drained from a big abscess formed in the groin between the peritoneum and the skin. He suspected this was caused from a ruptured appendix. He said I would probably have to carry a rubber drain in the incision to keep the cavity from filling up again.

The paralysis was caused from pressure the abscess was putting on the sciatic nerve, and as soon as the pressure was relieved, feeling started coming back in my leg. I got the first good nights sleep I had had in two months. The next morning when the corpsman came in to flush out the cavity, I was able to flex my leg a little. I felt so good and free of pain that I ate a hearty breakfast for the first time in weeks. On May 8, 1944, Captain Seid told me I was doing well enough to be moved out of the Hospital. He also said he thought I might have Tuberculosis, as he could hear something on the right lung. He put me in the TB ward, explaining that it was possible the abscess could be tubercular. It was still draining a lot and being flushed out every day.

During the time I was recuperating from the surgery, some Red Cross medicine was brought into camp. How long the Nips had been holding it is any one's guess. They were notoriously famous for receiving Red Cross goods and holding them to be dispensed in their own time. Who knows what an oriental is thinking. They are different, no doubt about it. There are some people who think it is their unique cultural differences, and we just did not understand them. All I can say is, try peddling that tripe to those poor Chinese they raped and murdered at Nanking Ask the many thousands of POWs who suffered first hand, the cruelty and inhumanity of the

Jap. They can relate story after story of brutality. Ask the Chinese, Filipinos, Koreans, Manchurians, and the many Dutch Indies folk and they all have stories of rape, murder and torture, too inhuman to imagine. What kind of 'unique culture' was it that produced soldiers like that?

Shortly after moving into the TB ward. I developed a case of diarrhea that defied all available medications. I lost my appetite completely, but forced myself to eat so I could keep much needed strength, only to either vomit it or have it run through me like water. During this time, I received a personal package from home that had been opened and repackaged. The contents did not come near matching the list of contents enclosed in the package. You would think if they were going to pilfer the contents and repackage them, they would at least remove the packaging list. But, what the hell did they care? The few things I did get I was able to eat and keep down. The sugar and powdered milk were a special Godsend. Whether it was the food from home or that the diarrhea had run its course, it started easing off. The cramping was not as severe and I wasn't going to the toilet as often. About this time they had another rest day and an overall weigh-in. I almost fell off the scales when I saw where the weight was placed. 44 kilometers. I could not believe it. I had heard of, read and scoffed at the "Charles Atlas" ads and the 97-pound man, and here I was, at 44 kilos, or a 97-pound weakling. I didn't dare look in a mirror for fear I would pass out at the sight of my own reflection. Heck, we had carried bodies weighing more than that to the cemetery in Cabanatuan. Then I realized just how sick I had been. As Captain Seid said after we'd been back in the states awhile; "You were just too dumb to die." And you know what, I think he was right. But ain't ignorance blissful? By June 10, 1944, the diarrhea had completely stopped and for the first time in nearly two months I could pass a solid stool.

Now that I could eat and keep it down, Captain put me on extra rations plus a canteen cup of soybean milk. We were getting a lot of soybeans now and one pot was put aside and cooked longer with more water. After the juice was dipped off, the beans were then mixed with the regular cooked beans. Captain Seid did not want to take the chance of my eating the beans yet, and I darn sure did not want to go through again what I had just been through. My side was still draining and the tailor had made another pad to hold the gauze in place so I always had a clean pad when the incision was dressed.

On June 10, 1944, several of the TB diagnosed patients were taken to the mill hospital for X-rays, along with little Jimmy Cole, who walked in a perpetual crouch. It was just another ruse to say they were observing the Geneva rules of war in the treatment of POWs. Captain Seid said that he could make out a small spot on my right lung, but it was not as bad as he thought, and it might or might not be Tuberculosis. The Japanese were dreadfully afraid of TB. As a result, we did not see much of the Jap hierarchy. We kept to our little corner in the front barracks, off limits to the camp.

The Japanese corpsman got the sneaky idea to take temperatures of all TB patients each morning. He had probably read or someone told him, persons with TB run fever most of the time. So the navy corpsmen came around each morning with a thermometer and took our temperature. Just before he was due, we sent over to the kitchen for a pot of tea. They had to keep a pot for the Jap all the time. We would sit around with a cup of tea until we saw the corpsman coming, at which time we dispensed with the cups and waited to see what our temperature would be after drinking the cup of hot tea. We were almost always running a fever. Even if the Japanese corpsman came along, we would be running a fever. Of course, the navy medic had a good idea what was going on. It was even rumored it was a navy corpsman's idea. I didn't know and did not want to know. It didn't last that long anyway.

On July 3, some Osaka doctors visited the camp to examine patients to be sent to the Kobe hospital for treatment. We were to be moved within the next 10 days, but by July 15 the whole thing had been called off. It was just another gesture to stay within the Geneva Convention rules. The food situation remained good and we were getting a wider variety of vegetables, some potatoes, soybeans, fish and some meat. So by the middle of July, when there was another rest day, I had gained 11 kilos, or 121 pounds. I am getting there.

On July 4, 1944, a second air raid alarm was sounded at the mill, but the next day the Japanese said it was not local. As if we were so dumb that we could not figure that out. The first alarm at the mill sounded February 8, 1944, but they said it was an accident due to a bad connection. The men coming in every day observed that bunkers and foxholes were being dug around the mill compound, and the guards were beginning to be a lot tighter and jumpier, initiating conservation with the POWs about bombing. They were feeling the iron claw closing. Since we were confined to the camp, what little news we received was brought in by our buddies. And, unless they were working an ore or coal boat, that news just might be rumor. Quite a bit could be learned from the crew of a ship if you could find one that was talkative. A lot of their crews were Koreans and Manchurians, pressed into service against their will, and they did not have any more love for the Japanese than we did.

During the month of July in 1944, several things happened to break the monotony of being cooped up in camp with nothing to do. The arrival of the men from work in the evening was always a source of new rumors. There were the rumors that all TB patients were to be put in a tuberculosis sanitarium in Kobe, but nothing ever came of it. There were rumors of how near the Allies were getting to Japan, and that food would be improving. This rumor proved to be 180 degrees off. We began to notice a shortage of green vegetables and soybeans in the soup, both of which had contributed so much to the overall general health of the POWs. The vegetables were our only source of vitamin C, without which we got sore mouths and throat and skin eruptions. The soybeans helped reduce the symptoms of Beri-Beri, to say nothing of adding a few pounds to our malnourished bodies.

The air raid sirens at the mill went off several times during July, and as always, the Japanese said they were exercises or false alarms. About the middle of the month, twelve Italian internees were brought into camp and housed separately from the POWs. We were informed, most emphatically, there would no mingling or communication with them. According to rumors, the internees were Italian merchant seamen and had been rescued when a Japanese submarine sunk their ship. As far as I know, no one ever saw them. If they were taken in and out of the camp, no one knew about that either.

Captain Seid had inserted a rubber drain in the incision in my back to keep it open, and decided to take it out and see if it would heal. It did not seem to be draining any more. This plan was short lived because less than twenty days after it had seemingly healed, I started running fever again and feeling pain in my groin. Within twenty-four hours, the incision ruptured and I awoke in a puddle of liquid, which leaked out of it. The corpsman was aroused, cleaned me up and reinserted the drain. Captain Seid told me the next day that I might as well figure on keeping that drain in until something else could be done about it, which, as it turned out, was until I got back to the states and had two surgeries to correct it.

July 26, 1944 was somewhat of a red-letter day for me. Although the twenty-one of us who were going to be transferred to Kobe hospital had our orders voided, we did get a nice surprise in the return of a patient named Wayne Smith from the Kobe Hospital. He had been sent to the Osaka Hospital in March, then transferred to the new Kobe Hospital in July. He reported it a nice, up-to-date hospital, with a library, hot and cold showers, tile bath, swimming pool and the works, but the food was lousy. (Sounds like some hospitals here in the good old USA) Up until the food assessment, it sounded like a good place to be sent. He also brought rumors of the Kobe bombing, Tojo's replacement and Japan sending an envoy to a conference in Russia. He said there was a Red Cross ship in Kobe harbor with Red Cross boxes and mail. Mail…the big morale lifter. I received two letters from home on 29 July, and though they were dated July and August 1943, a year earlier - letters were coming closer together. It was nice to know that my family was well. The month ended with all the rumors just being that, Rumors. To top it off, the Japanese had a shakedown of the barracks, confiscating salt, sugar, seasoning, removing all cigarettes from the TB ward and even turning some of the TB patients to duty and sending them out to work. That was their way of doing things, building your hopes all sky high and then cutting them down. Real little morale builders.

I Was There, Charley

Needless to say, the transfer never materialized. My thinking, it was another typical Japanese hoax all along.

The next few months of 1944 were, for all practical purposes, more of the same. As usual, the most interesting was what was brought in each day to be used as a food supply. We in the TB ward could look out the window toward the gate and watch the coming and going of all vehicles and what they were carrying. One day we saw the gates opened and in came a bull drawn, rubber tired wagon loaded with beef bone stripped of 99 percent of the meat. The dog pound would have had enough bones to feed 500 dogs or more. What do you do with a load of stinking, almost rotten beef bones? The cooks did the best they knew how without offending the Jap, if that was possible. They used hammer, cleavers and mallets to break the bones into small pieces, put them in a kawa of boiling water and cooked all the meat and marrow off and out of the bones, then steamed rice in the solution. The rice turned out a bit rancid, but at least it was packed with some protein and nutrients and was better than just plain rice. The next morning the wagon returned and hauled the used bones away. They probably still had some use for them.

Another day we watched as the wagon came with the largest solid piece of red meat imaginable. It had all the appearance of horsemeat, which we were introduced to on Bataan, but must have been at least four feet long by twenty-four inches in width and depth. It was too large for the kitchen door. Here is when the fun began: how to get a chuck of raw meat off that wagon and into the kitchen. From where we were, it looked like they cut it into large sections to get into the kitchen, then chopped in up into small chunks and cooked the chunks in the Kawas. That night we got three or four chunks of very tasty whale meat. It was much needed protein.

The strangest meat we ever received was brought in while I was still in the hospital after my surgery. We could smell it cooking when the odor wafted in from the direction of the kitchen. It smelled quite appetizing and had a definite fishy odor. That night, when the food was dished out, stacked in our mess kit on top of the rice was at least a teacup of some sort of ground meat. It definitely was some sort of sea animal, but the texture was not fish. We ate it with relish, so to speak, but for once I was not able to eat all of it, it was so rich. I felt full before I ordinarily would have. Then suddenly, one of the patients started vomiting. Two or three others said they felt like they were on fire they were so hot; their faces, arms and hands blood red. Some of them were having trouble breathing. This was happening in the barracks as well as the sickbay. Captain Seid was called and immediately declared it an allergenic reaction. The meat was octopus, which has a high protein and iodine content. Only a few of the men were affected who were highly sensitive to either the high protein content or the iodine. He suggested those having the problems try to upchuck it, if they hadn't already. He thought the malady would be short lived with no serious after affects. Sure enough, in most cases, everyone returned to normal, but that was the last octopus brought into camp.

We never knew the source of food coming into camp. Sometimes a truck would go to Kobe or Osaka and bring back a load of flounder or some other white fish. Sometimes, we were told, the mill was furnishing the food and other times the Japanese army took over the food supply. The one thing we were sure of was that it was never enough and always of questionable quality. I can see why they steam or boil all their food. With fecal matter for fertilizer and the way they handled raw meats and vegetables, steaming or boiling was the only way to avoid poison or bacterial contamination. Today, people are raving about Japanese cuisine. I wonder where it all was when I was their guest for three and a half years.

Sometime during 1944, I am not sure of the date, a big load of books with mostly English titles, arrived at our POW camp at Hirohata. Bill Hagedorn, one of the light duty patients and manager of the commissary and I instituted a library, setting up a borrowing system whereby the men could check out a book and read it at their leisure, if they had an urge to read. There was some good non-fiction, some do-it-yourself, travel, geography, Atlas and gobs of English who-done-its. I must have read well over a dozen who-done-its before I was shipped out to another camp a few months before the surrender.

We arrived in Japan in late fall. The barracks was new, with all new matting for bunks and I thought we were free at last of bedbugs and body lice so prevalent in Cabanbatuan. We had a larger space to call our own, with a small shelf at the head of our space on which to put our meager belongings. We were issued two regular size blankets and one long narrow blanket about two blanket lengths. We made what we called a "fart" sack out of them by laying the long narrow blanket from head to foot of the bunk area and leaving the excess rolled up at the foot. Then, by folding each regular blanket in half and laying the first blanket on the one on the matt and folding it out to the left and laying the second folded blanket on top of the first and folding it out to the right, folding the left back over the right blanket and folding the right half back over the left, finally pulling the part of the blanket on the mat up over the whole blanket pile, we made a sack-like affair to slip into when we retired, still having three layers under and three over. It was flexible and bent with you, and in the morning it was easy to slip out of and roll back up to the head of the bunk area where the Jap wanted it to be unless you were in it. A pillow you ask? We simply rolled up the jacket. That made a fine pillow. All the comforts of home.

I can safely say a working man spent most of the time he wasn't working in one of two places: the wash rack washing clothes or in his bunk area. There was nowhere else to go. You did not do much visiting because the Jap guards frowned on any gathering outside of barracks. They just did not want anyone loitering around the grounds. If you were outside, you had better be on our way to somewhere or on you way back to the barracks. The only place you could group was at the wash rack, and even that was constantly monitored. They did not miss a single way to make your life miserable. The minute you thought you had a comfort of sort, 'bingo,' they found a way to make you uncomfortable again. They had mastered that down to an art. Or maybe it was just that they had such an intense dislike for us and what we had and who we were.

I believe their treatment of the POWs remains a mystery to everyone who was ever involved. Some blame it on the Bushido code, which most Japanese officers adhered to and passed on down the chain of command. It was supposed to represent what the cadet at West Point is taught: Honor, courage, self-aggrandizement and respect. Where did all this cruelty, brutality and sadistic behavior come from? From all I saw and became a part of, on the Death March, at O'Donnell, Cabanatuan, in the two Japanese camps, and listening to stories from fellow POWs from other camps, the brutal and cruel treatment seemed to point to the fact that they were methodically and systematically eliminating the POWs under the guise of adhering to the Geneva Convention.

As in most cases where many bodies are crowded together in close confinement, there will be, even under the best of conditions, sanitation problems. In O'Donnell and at Cabanatuan, it had been body lice and bedbugs. This was a foregone conclusion, what with little water, dirty sleeping conditions, no change of clothes and the close proximity of bodies; however, we expected better in Japan. It was a new camp, cleaner with facilities for bathing and washing clothes far superior to those we had just left. Since it was late fall when we arrived, we settled in and everything was going along fine until the weather warmed and something biting us. The first thing we thought about was the bedbugs in the Philippines, but a diligent search found none. Still, we were scratching all night long and getting very little sleep. When I had to go to the Hospital I was not bothered with the biting. Further pursuit of the problem finally paid off: the camp was built so close to the shoreline the topsoil was sandy and full of sand fleas. Many hours of sleep were lost until one innovative POW, working the naphthalene plant, got the idea of putting naphthalene flakes in his bed. Voila! It worked. It kept the sand fleas out of his "fart-sack." Others tried it until the barracks smelled like a mothball factory. The Jap, making one of their usual inspections, smelled the naphthalene and wanted to know why. When we told him, instead of blowing his stack as we expected, he seemed to be quite elated and rushed to the office to report it, whereupon the commandant came out and, after a thorough explanation, returned to his office. The next day a load of naphthalene flakes were brought into camp and put on the floor underneath the bunks. Not only in our quarters but in the Jap quarters as well. Seems the sand fleas were not all that particular whose body they nibbled on. The only negative aspect was the mothball smell, but for a good nights sleep you can do most anything. I am glad I left before the next spring came around. Fleas must hibernate in the winter.

During the time I was at Hirohata, we were allowed three church services. If I remember right the first one was a Japanese Baptist minister. We were required to attend the services. The guards herded us into a barracks and the minister stood at one end of the aisle, delivered his sermon in most precise English, finished and immediately left. Whether he had orders not to make conversation with anyone or whether he just wanted to get out of there, we never knew, but we suspected he had orders to conduct the service and get out as fast as he could. The next service was from a Japanese Catholic priest. We'd had a change in command between the two services, and the new commandant allowed the priest to talk to those of us who wanted to talk to him. He did not venture any news and the catholic men respected his position, not questioning him along that line. These required services were always conducted in the same place, and we wondered at the lenient position of the Japanese commandant. We later found out from the Japanese interpreter that the commandant was also Catholic. We'd talked about the new commandant after he had been there awhile, and noted he was not as hardnosed as the ones before him, and made definite attempts to improve the food situation. Whether his being Catholic had anything to do with these actions would be only conjecture on my part, but I think it was. The next pastor was Japanese also and a Methodist. The services went much the same as the other two, with his saying very little to the POWs and being ushered out promptly by the guards when he finished.

While I was in the TB ward, we had a lot of time to kill and since the library was going, I did quite a bit of reading. I read one book on 'Radio Script Writing,' which interested me. Of course, I had a lot of use for it in my position. I read another '20th Century Locomotives,' which was easy reading and mostly all pictures. I began giving the British 'Who Done Its' a going over. It took some of those authors a long time to get into a story, setting the scenes, introducing the characters etc. You almost lost interest before you got into the book, but after it started, it moved pretty fast, was suspenseful, had a good plot and made for good reading.

During these times I was able to keep what boudoir I owned, clean by washing clothes every day. Gave me something to do. Hutch Gardener, a good friend from my hometown took me under his wing when I was so sick with diarrhea. I wanted so much to do something for him, so I asked if I could wash his clothes. He was reluctant at first, but I insisted and started doing a few pieces for him now and then. Later, he gave me an old cardigan he had about worn out to see if I could use it. Cardigans, like vests, have no sleeves. I looked it over and thought I could get enough good cloth out of it to make some sleeves for an old cardigan I had that was not so badly worn. I fashioned a pattern out of some wrapping paper I found in the Commissary office and made several modifications to the pattern before daring to cut the cloth. It took me three days to make the first sleeve, but after I got the bugs ironed out, I made the next sleeve in one day. Then came the day of revelation…would the sleeve fit the opening in the cardigan. I must have been living right. It was not the problem I had anticipated. The needle I used was so big and the thread so heavy, it took forever to get the stitches in, but once there, they were not going anywhere and would be there for a long time. I had made a fair looking jacket, all English wool, and it was warm. I planned to bring it home for a souvenir when we were liberated. The Navy corpsman who was processing us on the Navy Hospital ship after we were liberated, however, told me to pitch it on an already large pile of discarded clothes. He said it would make a good fire in the ships furnace. In other words since the ship used oil for heating, he was telling me they didn't want all those rags on the ship. Oh well, you can't win them all.

During the month of September 1944, there were constant rumors of Germany taking a beating in Europe. Paris was retaken, British and American troops had the Germans on the run. There was supposed to have been a rather recent copy of a British newspaper circulating in camp. Must have been some truth, because the Medical corpsman had the duty for that week and was running the workers after the evening meal for no reason at all. He even had all men stand out in the courtyard until 11:30 waiting for someone to turn the paper over to him. He finally went to bed and the first sergeant dismissed the men. He was afraid there would be repercussions from the Jap Corpsman for dismissing the men, but nothing was ever said about it. A few days' later, rumors were floating around about the fall of Formosa and the U.S. troops taking Takao. The Corpsman went on a rampage again. He was such a perverted bastard that he used any excuse to punish the POWs in many sadistic ways. We'd heard he was injured in the Coral Sea battle so badly that he was given a medical discharge which, according to the Bushido code, is a 'No, No'…you are supposed to die for the emperor. Maybe because of his disgrace, he took it out on any one under his command and most especially the POWs, blaming us for his inadequateness. To make matters worse, it rained most of the month of September. Maybe this could account for his foul mood. In any case, he seemed to stay in a rainy mood.

During this period and on into October, the food situation varied from day today. One day, feast, the next day famine. Let me qualify the word "feast:" very little better than the usual. I have heard the average daily food allotment for all camps was 750 grams for working men, 500 for light duty and 350 for the sick. At Hirohata the sick were reduced to one-half rations, but that was all figured in to the amount the Japanese Quartermaster doled out to the kitchen each day. The kitchen, which was manned by POWs, put it all in the pots, cooked it and doled it out to each man equally. Thus, if the sick were cut, the whole camp took up the slack. Whether the Jap knew we were doing it that way or not, I have no way of knowing, but to my knowledge they never ever said anything one way or the other. At Hirohata, the rations were determined by calories allowed: 1200 for workers, 800 for light duty and 500 for the sick. So, according to those estimates, no one in the camp got the 1200 but by the same token no one received the 500.

The weather in Japan is constant. Constantly bad. Too hot or too cold, too wet or too dry. Starting in September, it rains or looks like rain three-fourths of the time, even into the winter months when you have cold with rain and an occasional snow, at least in the area around Osaka bay. This makes for miserable working conditions, and we worked every day, rain or shine. It seemed like, starting in November through March and April, the only time you were ever warm was the nights we were able to take a warm bath. There was no heat anywhere at the mill unless you happened to be nearby when they stacked some freshly poured iron slabs out in the yard. Then you could feel the heat for 10 of 15 feet from that location. The barracks were, for all practical purposes, heatless. One stove might heat a 10-foot radius of it, and the remainder might be 5 degrees warmer than outside. The summer, being on the coastline, was hot and humid. In spite of the netting, mosquitoes and sand fleas played havoc with your ability to sleep. We finally curtailed the flea activity and it seemed to affect the mosquitoes so they were not as bad. The windows were left open, but since a solid 10-ft wooden fence surrounded the compound, there was very little breeze. Fortunately, after working all day at the mill, no one had to rock you to sleep at night.

During October and November there were daily rumors of the European campaign, about the taking back of Paris and the Germans on the run. On October 10 came the rumor that the Siegfried line had broken and the allies were in Berlin. Also, that Russian troops had broken through on the eastern front. Then on Oct. 16, the complete collapse of the German army and unconditional surrender. On the 21st, rumors had it that all China was in allied hands, Luzon and Formosa in American hands. Japanese officials and guards were getting a little hard-nosed and looking for anything to make trouble. It all added up. At the time, we had no way of confirming any of these rumors, but after it was all over, we realized some of these rumors were not so far off. At this time, I was still doing light duty and the Corpsman was still trying to get 400 men out to the mill each day, even if he had to take men out of the sick bay to do it. I was lucky, and escaped his wrath, and at the same time I worked myself into a sort of business. After I made the jacket out of a cardigan, other guys wanted to know if I could do this and that and most of the time I could, and was doing quite a bit of sewing and tailoring. I did laundry for the medics and they paid me in credits they had at the commissary. The workers were getting paid now, but it was all on paper. They were given a certain amount of credit at the commissary and they could take it out in trade such as salt, pepper, ginger, and other odds and ends. Since I was on light duty, I did not get paid, nor did any of the patients in the TB ward or sick bay, so this was my way of building up a commissary account. I washed or sewed, and the commissary manager transferred the amount I charged for a service from the customer's account to mine. Would you believe, I got home with my account book…quite a cherished item now.

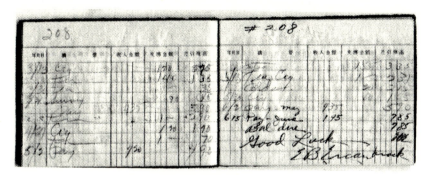

Page from Commissary Book

November 1944 was a month of rumors and rain. Under the best of conditions the weather in Japan would be classified as terrible, but this was the most miserable weather imaginable, even for Japan. Most of the rumors centered around the progress of the Allies in their closing in on Japan. Most days and nights there were air raid sirens and Japanese planes were sighted occasionally, but so far we hadn't seen any high flying bombers, even though rumors had them making repeated raids on Osaka, Kobe, Yokohama and Tokyo. Some rumors had Japan and the USA signing a peace treaty and us moving out in a next few days, but by the end of the month it was still the same old food, work, promised rest days and the usual status quo. The only rumor that panned out after the November presidential election in the States was Roosevelt being reelected as President and that made the Japanese very unhappy. He was the one reason there was no peace treaty. They blamed him for everything, just as we blamed everything on Tojo.

I passed my 28 birthday on November 7 and some of my buddies in the TB ward gave me a birthday party. We had received some Red Cross boxes the day before and sort of lived it up, with one box divided between two men. A can of Spam divided between eight men is really living it up. We had all the green tea we could drink, but then tea was always available if you wanted it. In this case, we had a bit of powdered milk and sugar to go with it, topped off with a handful (small hand) of raisins for dessert. Armistice day was just another day, even though it had been rumored to be the signing of the treaty between Japan and the USA.

After an air raid warning the night of November 27, the workers were put to working on air aid shelters at the mill. It seemed the (B-ni-ju-kyu) B-29s were getting too close for comfort. The next night was hot bath night and the Jap Medical Corpsman took his frustrations or sadistic tendencies out on the TB ward and the Sick bay by refusing them permission to bathe. We have no idea what bought on his ranting, but he paraded up and down, banging on the rails of our bunk with his swagger stick for a good fifteen minutes, finally striding off, screaming in English. "No bath, No Bath." What it was all about, nobody knew.

All month we looked forward to Thanksgiving and the rumors of 'Takusan' (much) food. Well, for once the rumors turned out on the affirmative side. Red Cross boxes were issued before breakfast. This would have been a treat in itself, but the Jap must have opened the doors to the warehouse and said, 'help yourself.' For once, by turning in all the coffee from the Red Cross boxes to the kitchen, we had coffee all day if we wanted it. There were extra rations of rice, beans, sweet potatoes, and the old standby, greens. A real treat was the tangerine given to each man. I traded American cigarettes for a couple of tangerines. There was usually a lot of trading going on when we did get a Red Cross box. The only negative side of the day was the cold wind that blew all day, and some of the men were put to work, in shifts, digging air raid shelters in the compound to be used by the Jap. Otherwise, it was a Royal day in Nippon.

Among the many diseases, maladies etc that beset the POWs were carbuncles, boils and sties, which seemed to appear with any change of diet. I first noticed my first boil after the Red Cross boxes were issued in Cabanatuan, then again in Hirohata in the latter part of 1944, when we started getting bulk Red Cross food and more personal boxes. I have never found anyone who could give me an answer. They only say these are caused from infection. I mentioned this to Captain Seid after a siege of boils and sties during November and December 1944 and the early 1945 when I had sties on both eyes at one time, almost leaving me and in total darkness. In all, I had three of these on the left eye and one on the right eye and at the same time I had boils on both lower limbs along the shin bone, and two or three on my buttocks. These were very painful and made it almost impossible to get around. Captain Seid just thought it was some sort of staph infection.

Only a few POWs were afflicted by these boils, but one of those was a friend of mine who was sent to sick bay because he could not stand any weight on his right leg and still work. He had three boils on the shin area of that leg. I watched the corpsman dress the wound as he ran a piece of medicated gauze in one hole left by the boils and bring it out the hole of another. For a time, they were afraid he might loose his lower left limb, fearful it would develop into gangrene. A Japanese doctor from Osaka said it was Chinese Rot or jungle rot, but offered no treatment. It must have run its course, because for no reason at all the swelling reduced and the wounds became less inflamed; eventually healing completely, leaving ugly scars. Yet the majority of the men suffered no such manifestations. The strange thing about it was I had never had a boil. The corpsmen were extremely cautious in seeing that the dressings got nowhere near the open incision in my book.

Christmas 1944 finally arrived. We'd heard numerous rumors as to what would be on the menu, one rumor having us being liberated by then and on our way home. Air raid warnings were a daily occurrence, and some days we had as many as two or three. On one day the workers were called off the job and brought home This was the same day it was rumored that Kobe, Osaka and Tokyo, all were hit. I think at this time the U.S. air corps was dropping incendiary bombs in the form of a large bomb filled with what looked like many

18 inch aluminum cylinders about 2 to 3 inches in diameter. The small bombs were filled with napalm, a jelly-like gasoline substance similar to the substance the allied troops were using to drive the Jap out of the caves on the various islands in the pacific. It is jelly-like and sticks to anything it hits and burns at several hundred degrees. When I changed camps in June, riding in a truck up through Osaka and Kobe, everything as far as you could see was burned to the ground except for concrete and steel buildings. Piled up along the way in stacks were the aluminum cylinders that had contained the napalm.

Christmas day came and went without any air raid alarms. The Air Corps was giving their crews a day off. This Christmas day was much improved over the ones of 1942 and 1943. I wrote in my diary that I hoped the next Christmas would be spent at home, and, sure enough, I was at least back in the good old USA even though I was confined to an Army Hospital in Santa Fe, New Mexico. Arriving in late September 1945, I was put in the TB isolation ward for the next four months. During that time all my family could and did come up to see me. The food this Christmas was not as good as at Thanksgiving, because the Red Cross boxes and food promised was not delivered. For no reason other than the Japanese were just being Japanese. Or it could have been for lack of transportation as they claimed. The answer is anyone's guess, but I guess they did it on purpose and gloated over it. Regardless, it was a nice and warm day with no work. A short morning Christmas service was conducted by one of the older prisoners who, at one time, had aspired to be a Baptist preacher. I thought under the circumstances it was as appropriate as any Christmas I had attended in the past. Here we had a man under the direst of circumstances, preparing and conducting a Christmas service that spoke loudly of peace on earth, good will to all men. He spoke from the heart and we listened from the heart. It was truly a unique experience.

After deciding to do this book, I started perusing my many notebooks and my diary for details and dates. In the course of moving from place to place, I either did not keep a diary from January 1,1945 until June 17, 1945 when I was transferred from Hirohata to Fusiki

POW camps, or I have lost pages. I still have the little notebook on which I kept an accounting of my days at Fusiki. So I will resort to the old noggin and see what comes up. This shouldn't be hard, as the time span was short and the memories mostly all pleasant, if not enjoyable, as we could begin to see the end. But first I will try to remember my last days at Hirohata.

The air raid alarms became more numerous and the Japanese more itchy. They were in between the rock and the hard place .At that time we did not know the Japanese supreme command had sent out specific orders to all prison camp commandants that, in case of invasion, all POWs were to be eliminated and he gave explicit instruction as to how it was to be carried out. Had I have known this, I would have been a little more apprehensive about my welfare. As it was, we knew only that it was a matter of time. We were so overjoyed by the thought of liberation that we could not possibly be aware of the many perils we might encounter on our way to that goal.

I was left in sickbay where I'd gone with my boils problems, and left there because of an indigestion problem that did not seem to improve. I had a constant sort of hungry feeling in my stomach that became painful after eating. I was nauseous a lot to the time to the point that I did not feel up to eating and when I did eat, I had that pain in my stomach. I'd never had ulcers, nor knew anyone who had, but I could imagine how they might feel. Capt. Seid didn't think that it was ulcers, but put me on a soymilk diet and told me to lay off the Red Cross food when offered. This was quite a come down, but I took the good Doctor's advice and the malady did get better. I was just getting to the point where I though I was cured, when I'd be moved back to the TB ward. Several of the men were coming down with something resembling meningitis, and this being a very contagious disease, moved everyone out of sick bay, putting new patients in for observation, isolating them from everyone except the corpsmen who attended them. They were ordered to wear masks when in the sick bay and to wash everything after coming out. At this time I weighed 66 kilos (145 pounds)

Feeling much better, I went back on the regular rice and soup diet and tolerated it quite well. I resolved to leave that rich Red Cross food alone, but I did not have to worry because I never saw a Red Cross box or any Red Cross food after that. I was put back on light duty status and did light camp cleanup. This meant cleaning the wash racks, swabbing out the toilets, helping in the kitchen when needed and helping unload the wagons and trucks when they came with food and other odd and ends. At other times, I did little chores for the 'working' men, and read some. I went back to helping Hegedorn in the commissary and library when he wanted to take an hour or two off

Captain Seid hadn't taken my drain out for some time now, and things seemed to be going pretty well. I had enough other things plaguing me that I about decided my side was healed up for good. I discarded the pads with the strings attached, used to hold the gauze in place, because I thought my problem there was solved. But I gloated too soon. Around the first of February 1945, I began to feel achy and sort of washed out. I didn't think I was working all that hard, so I tried to shrug it off and go on about my daily chores. Then I got the feeling I was running a fever, and at night I would wake up sweating. On the morning of February 15, it was all I could do to make myself get up. When Diedrich, the Corpsman, came to take our temperature, mine was 102 degrees. He looked at me and asked if the tea was too hot and grinned. I knew what he was referring to and told him I had not even had any tea. Then he reached over and put his hand on my forehead, then took off for the office. Five minutes later, Capt Seid showed up and did the same thing, asking me if my side hurt. I had not thought about it, but it was a little tender. He laid me back and probed with his hand saying he was afraid the abscess had filled up again and he'd have to open and drain it again. By this time, the Japanese had supplied the medics with some Novocaine for injuries sustained on the job. He injected this around the incision and lanced it again, drawing off another half pan of pus. He said he had to put the drain back in and for me to wear it continuously until I could have an appendectomy to remove the old appendix that was sloughing off. He then put some gauze over it and stuck it down with a couple of pieces of adhesive tape.

Then he went with me to the tailor shop and told them to make me two more pads with strings so I could have one on and one in the wash and dry. Then I went back to work doing the same thing until I was shipped out June 19 1945 to where…to parts unknown.

During this time, rumors had it again that Germany had surrendered, only this time it was for real. This was May 6, 1945, the same time that 134 men were sent off camp on detail. This has always been a question in my mind. I have seen accounts of them being sent out on a temporary detail. If that is true, they never returned – at least not while I was still there. If they were sent somewhere else, I have never seen any account of where they were sent. Aside from that, less than three weeks later, a group of 30 were sent out and I was in that group. The Japanese medical corpsman got to clean out the sickbay and TB ward, because those were the members making up detail.

Clemens A. Kathman

CHAPTER SIX
FUSIKI CAMP JUNE 23, 1945--SEPTEMBER 5, 1945

June 23, 1945, as the 30 of us piled into the back of an old dilapidated truck, was a nice morning, but already showed signs of becoming another hot day. We headed for who knows where. It could be better than what we were leaving, or vice versa; but in our situation we had very little to say about it. I can't say I was happy about the situation, as I had rather stayed in Hirohata. Like the lady who was changing doctors, I felt I was in good hands with someone familiar with my case, though it wasn't the best place in the world to be at that time. At least I knew and was content with the status quo.

Captain Seid had written a complete history of my ailments and treatments to be given to the doctor or doctors in the camp to which I might be going. He had the tailors make another couple of pads with straps and more gauze pads to be washed out daily and sanitized with chlorinated lime. The lime he had packaged up in small packets to be used each time I washed the pads and gauze. He then, like any good doctor, passed on instructions: if, ands. and buts that might occur down the line. Then to my biggest surprise, gave me a big hug, told me would see me back in New Mexico and jokingly remarked "You are here today, only because you were to dumb to die." Afterward, he continued in a more serious tone, "I don't think you ever realized how really sick you were." Many times in the past sixty some years I have recalled what he said and each time, I am sure, had it not been for his perseverance and care, I would not be here today. In my opinion, Captain Sidney E. Seid is one unsung hero. Doctor, I salute you.

We arrived at a staging area in Kobe later in the day after passing through some of the most devastated area the human mind could possibility imagine. For miles and miles through Osaka and into

Kobe there was nothing but barren, landscape burned black from the thousands of napalm bombs dropped on it. An occasional concrete building could be seen standing. Steel girders lay crisscrossed on the ground, the wooden structures burned from under them. Heavy machinery could be seen amid the burned rubbish denoting that what was supposed to have been homes were actually small manufacturing plants set up in those habitations. Japan had geared up everything to be used in their war effort. If there had been any doubt of why the U.S. bombers had bombed civilian area, the display of all those high precision industry tools and machinery, strewn among the burned-out homes, was reason enough. Most of Japan's homes were little better than bamboo frames covered with paper or some other flammable material and burned like kindling. I am afraid at that point in time we could not work up much sympathy for the inhabitants.

After we had been settled into what appeared to have been barracks on an army post, we were told we might be there for a few days as groups from other camps would be joining us later. Evidently we must have been the first group to arrive. That night we received a more than adequate meal. We had not eaten since that morning at 6 a.m. and were beginning to think they did not feed in these parts. They had an early evening call and we bedded down on bamboo slats with straw mats. That was it. We had turned in all bedding when we left Hirohata, now all we had were the clothes on our backs. The three days we were there, food was all we received. That was a novelty. It was the same old, same old, but more of it. That, in itself, was an improvement. Was this an indication that, just maybe, things were going to get better?

I had my first try at dressing the incision in my back. I was not sure, if I got the rubber drain out, I could get it back in right.. I did as Captain Seid told me, first mixing a small amount of the chlorinated lime with water in the canteen cup. Then, removing the gauze pad, I poured some of the liquid over it, rinsed it out under the faucet. Afterward, I removed the drain and did the same with it. I then took the pad with the straps and rinsed them, pouring some of the lime solution over it and washing the area around the wound. With a clean gauze pad and strap assembly, I was ready to replace the rubber tube. It slipped in easily and went only so far, relieving my mind of the possibility of it going in too far and not being able to get it out again. On went the strap harness and the gauze pad under it and I was back in business once more. This routine was done every night until I went aboard the Navy hospital ship September 5, 1945.

The next day, we were up at 6 a.m. and lined up outside for some morning wake up exercises. The night had not been all that bad. A couple of pit calls as per usual and waking up two or three times to change positions and keep the slats from burrowing up in our skin and the little flesh you had on the aching bones. That was a good nights sleep. After the exercises, the Jap guard picked me and another guy and we went to the kitchen and got the morning rations of rice and seaweed soup with what appeared to be small pieces of fish in it and a bucket of warm green tea. We returned, rationed it equally among the men and enjoyed a quiet breakfast, while contemplating what the day had in store. Suspense, with the Japanese it is always suspense. We washed the buckets and returned them to the kitchen and prepared to make the best of another day.

We did not have long to wait. About midmorning three truck loads of some of the worst mutilated people I had ever seen arrived. Most of them looked as if big area of their skin had been ripped off. They had very little clothing on. In fact, I found out that they could not stand the touch of clothing on those horrible looking sore all over their bodies. We were told they had been imprisoned down in the Kobe dock area when the B-29s had first bombed Kobe using the napalm incendiary bombs. They had to fight their way out of the barracks to get to area that was not burning. Many of them had the napalm jelly-like substance splattered on them and in attempting to wipe it off, only spread it over a wider area of their body, still burning. This had happened more than a month before, and the Jap were now moving these more mobile cases out of the makeshift hospital. I can just imagine the appearance of those cases left in the hospital. They said that many of the men there, to sick to move on their own, were burned to a crisp. They did not know how many were killed but most all of them had received burns to some degree. The lesser burned POWs were still down there, moved to new quarters, but working.

One fellow, who took the area beside me on the upper bay, had several small spots of burned flesh on his arms and legs that were healing nicely, and two real ugly burns were on each arm. He said that when he finally got out of the burning barracks, everything around him was ablaze. His first thought was to head for the dock and dive in the water, as that was really the only place he could see that wasn't burning. So he took it. There were burning bodies running every which way. All of a sudden he heard a loud pop close by and the next thing he knew he was covered with fire. He had had the presence of mind to pick up his musette bag and throw it over his shoulder, his only other covering being a G-string. It was June and already hot at night in the Kobe-Osaka area.

When he felt the stuff hit him, he knew the worst spots were the two on his arms, so he reached back and got the musette bag, using it to swab the burning gel off. The bag just smeared the gel on down his arm almost to his hand, leaving gel burning in its wake. Then he wiped the other arm with the same results. He kept swatting at the flames with the bag until he either put it out or it burned itself out, he didn't know which. The small spots on his lower limbs must have burned themselves out when he realized he was hurting all over. He had got past most of the fire, and came to the corner of a building that had a large concrete barrel of water on each corner, which the Jap use in case of fires. He said he just jumped in and sat there until they found him the next morning. Trying to get out just bought on the pain. Sitting in the water, he said, he could at least live with it. Later on in the makeshift hospital, the Japanese smeared the burned area with a thick smelly ointment. Then he found out how badly he had been burned, and that there were others even burned a lot worse than he was. He had a solid scab on both arms that ran from the middle of the upper arm all the way down to the top of the hand, plus a dozen or more spots on his legs the size of the eraser on a pencil. These were almost healed. There were several spots on his head where the gel had burned through the hair to the skin. We all kept our hair clipped, so that was not a lot of hair. He said the Japanese doctor told him the hair would not grow back in those spots. After we got to Fusiki, he did light work in the kitchen and was beginning to get back to normal when we were liberated. I decided right there I would not trade places with him.

Nothing much happened the rest of that day. We sort of lay around and shot the breeze, waiting for the next meal and observing the sights. The encampment was situated in the foothills away from the dock area, surrounded by homes that appeared to be suspended in the air on the side of the steep hills. Big, nice, affluent homes not so far away but that we could see action in and about the houses. Seeing what we assumed were maids and yardmen working the yards, you would never know there was a war going on. Not from the appearance on the hill. There was this, what appeared to be, Anglo woman that stood out on the balcony of the house and combed her hair each morning. The last morning we were there we lived dangerously and waved at her. Sure enough, she waved back. The next day we were on out way aboard a train for who knew where? Another surprise or just another hell hole.

Each day saw a new group of POWs come into the compound, all in much the same condition as we were. Nearly all of them had been riding the sick list of the camp from which they were sent. Every one of these camps were reducing their number to get it down to where they could better handle the POWs in case of another emergency like the one at Kobe.

I Was There, Charley

Picture of the Eleven Nationalities in Fusiki

The day we were to be shipped out, a group came in that looked healthier and in better shape physically. It was made up of prisoners taken from Singapore, including men from Great Britain, Australia, Dutch Indies, China, Turkey, Egypt, Greece, India, Philippines, Spain and Ireland. Some 75 or 80 were Englishmen from the Singapore garrison. The Australians and Dutch were captured on Java, the other eight nationalities were made up of British merchant seaman who had been picked up when their ships were sunk by the Japanese or German submarines. They were a rough and tough looking lot.

That night, as a group of us who were sleeping on the upper bay were getting ready to turn in, a group of Limeys (English) were underneath us and were chattering like a bunch of magpies, dropping their 'H's' all over the place. They were presumed to be speaking English, but you could hardly understand a word they were saying. One kept saying something about the Queen. When he finished, two or three popped up with "God Bless the Queen." One our guys piped out with "and while you're at it, "Bless Uncle Sam." I don't think he expected them to even hear him. I never saw five men move as fast as those Limeys did. They came out from under that bay cussing a blue streak. One caught me by the foot, twisting and pulling at the same time trying to remove me from where I was seated. With the other foot, I kicked him on the forehead, sending him tumbling into the bay across the aisle. The other four were trying to get up in the upper bay, but were being kept down by the other guys in our group.

From out of nowhere, seemingly, two big hulks started grabbing those Limeys as if they were cordwood, pushing them back into the bay under us, demanding to know what this was all about. It was over as fast as it began. This one big guy with a dozen hash marks on his shirt turned to me and asked, "Well Mate, what is this all about?" I told him all I knew, then he turned to one of the Limeys and asked him the same question. The Limey told him we had insulted the Queen. He turned back to me and explained that these people held the Queen in the highest regard and any insult about her is an insult to Great Britain. "What we have here," he said, " is lack of communication." I agreed with him and told him we felt the same way about Uncle Sam. That we felt, very strongly, an allegiance to all our allies and respected the Queen as much as we did Roosevelt, our president and that we held her in equal respect. With that, he climbed up in the bunk with us and introduced himself. His name was "Pug" Barron and he was a WO1, or warrant Officer, in her majesty's forces in the Far East. He gave me his outfit and first name, but all anyone ever called him was 'Pug.' His partner was William Poulter, also a WO1. Both had been in the far east command for dozens of years and hardly spoke like the English. His men were all Englishmen from a part of London similar as to Brooklyn is to New York, and this was his comparison. Their distinctive speech was characteristic of these people, sort of like 'Eliza' in 'My Fair Lady.' Three or four of us shot the breeze until the Jap came through and told us to go to bed. We would be leaving early the next morning.

I Was There, Charley

Bill Poulter

We took the truck down to the railroad station, which was concrete and still standing because it was concrete. Unlike the Philippine train ride, this train had seats like the one on the trip from Moji to Hirohata. Narrow, but comfortable. By this time many of the men in our group ran into men they had known and been associated with back in the Philippines. It sort of like old home week as they had been separated sometime since they had become prisoners, and had not seen each other in several months and sometimes years.

Most of them, getting together again, gathered together in the same car. I was the only one from my group of friends and associates shipped out of Hirohata not running into anyone I knew. I must have looked lost as I wondered down the aisle of the car, looking for a familiar face. When I got to the end of the car, I heard some one sing out, "Hey, Mate, wait up." I turned around and found myself staring into the face of my British friend of the night before. "We have a couple of empty seats up front, why don't you join us?" he asked. So that's how I got stuck with the Brits, Aussies and the rest of the mixed Singapore bunch. Not that I minded one bit. They were as nice a bunch of 'Blokes as you would want to be associated with.

The ride to Fusiki was uneventful. There were several stops, one in which bentos (lunch boxes) were brought aboard and each of us given one. It was not much, but it was good. Also some green tea was distributed throughout the cars. I guess we must have been as curious to the Japanese as they were to us. Most of them had never seen an Anglo and we darn sure had never been Japan. It is quite a picturesque island. Even during the war years it still had its beauty spots as well as some strange sites. We passed through parts of Nagoya, or that is what we were told. The part we saw looked like Kobe and Osaka. Mile after mile was dotted with rubble left by bombs from American bombers. Here we saw the result of heavier bombs because large stone, brick and metals building were totally destroyed.

Then we coasted back into the countryside and everything was quite, as if there were no war at all. Finally, late in the afternoon, the train started backing up and we were ordered to get our gear and get off. We were conducted into one of the most dilapidated quarters I ever expect to occupy. They had taken a couple of old warehouses and converted them into barracks with upper and lower bays with pine boards for bunking space. The buildings were well constructed to endure the strain of the many earthquakes to which Japan is constantly subjected. They had tile roofs, but for all practical purposes there was very little ventilation. They'd converted another small building into a kitchen with equipment to outfit it. A 10-foot heavy wood fence surrounded it with a double gate at the front and a guardhouse with a jail just inside the gate. The barracks had dirt floors and you could see daylight between the planks that served as walls. The first thing that entered my mind was I hope we don't have to spend a winter here. Sure enough, we didn't.

An evening meal of rice and the old standby, greens soup was ready when we arrived. But we had to wait, what seemed to be two or three hours as we were divided into groups of 50 men. There were enough Americans to make three groups of 50 men each with six left over. There were enough British to make two groups of 50 each with 12 left over. The Dutch had enough for one group and several over. They then took the extra American, Brits, Turks, Greeks, and Aussies and made another group of 50. With the Dutch and all the other nationalities making up the sixth group of 50. I was in the group with the Brits, Aussies, Turks, and Greeks. Then they started looking for cooks. Seems everyone wanted to be a cook. Naturally. They ate best. We were all assigned barracks according to groups,. and finally ordered to fall out for mess. We formed a line with mess kit and canteen cup and a group of, what appeared to be Japanese civilians dished out the food. There was more than we had been getting at Hirohata, but you never get your hopes too high. You just take it one meal at a time and hope you get one.

While we were eating, I was setting with Pug and Bill, the two WO1s, and I just made the remark, I wonder who will be the Allied man in command. We did not have any officers that I knew off. It was then that I found out there was a British doctor in the group who would probably be put in charge. While we were eating, the doctor was having lunch with the Japanese commander and his crew. Later on another British WO1 was called into the office. The next morning we found out the WO1 had been put in charge of the camp. The doctor had declined the responsibility and suggested the WO1 be make the allied commander. I was standing in line behind Pug and Bill when I heard Pug say, real low, to Bill. "Once a cunt, always a cunt." I thought to myself the American meaning of that word. I didn't think it was complimentary by the tone of Pug's voice.

The WO1 began explaining what was about to happen, and what the future held for us. He asked each group to get together and elect a leader and assistant, preferably a senior non-commissioned officer, and meet with him in his office at 0900. There would be no work that day. We would be issued blankets and mats later in the day plus a roll of toilet paper for each man. We were all just about afoot and would be getting a pair of "tabi" (a canvas shoe resembling a high top tennis shoe) The doctor would be holding sick call in his office (the doctor and the WO1 had quarters and offices together.) later in the day. All men able to walk would be expected to go to work. Any man who thought he couldn't work should see the doctor. Men on the sick list would be getting half rations. I guess he thought that would keep the men from making sick call. But some of the men I saw looked like stretcher cases and putting them on half rations was not going to accomplish anything.

I made sick call only to show the doctor the note that Capt. Seid had given me. I believed I was strong enough to work and was going to try it. The Doctor read the note and shook his head, frowned and asked me what I wanted to do, telling me he didn't think I should be doing what we were going to be doing. Then I found out what we would be doing. Stevedore work. About as hard work as there is, but it might be hard to keep me in camp as I appeared to be in pretty good shape, but he would try. I told him I wanted to try to work if I could, so he marked me for duty, but told me to keep in touch. That was the last time I saw him. I don't even remember seeing him when we departed the place. When I got back from sick call, both Pug and Bill, who, incidentally, our squad had elected our leader and assistant leader, asked how it went. I told them I was going to work, then they told me about the doctor. They intimated he was gay. (they were not so kind) and they were not too sure of the WO1. I heard them use the word 'cunt' many times after that, and came to the conclusion that it was a derogatory way of describing someone as a 'no-good-nik.' But the English have many terms they use that is confusing until you have been around them for awhile.

The new cooks, preparing meals that morning and considering their experience or lack of it, did a pretty good job. The WO1 put one of the burn victims from Kobe as mess sergeant, as that was his job in the 59th CAC, I think. Most of the help in the kitchen had had experience at one time or another. To keep the able-bodied burn victim in camp, they worked in the kitchen or camp detail. There were many of the burn victims and those who came with me from Hirohata were so badly burned there was no way could they be expected to do stevedore work. But then the next morning when we fell out for work. I was wondering how many we would be carrying back in that afternoon.

There was a Japanese garrison down the road from our camp that furnished the guards for the camp. Their commander was the commandant of the prison camp. We fell in by squads and marched in the same order. 1st squad first, 2nd Squad second, and so on. One Jap in the lead, four to six along each side and one bring up the rear kept us in step. We marched in columns of four. It was probably a mile or more to the dock area. We walked in and walked back. We went to work at 8 a.m. and quit at 5 p.m. with a 30-minute lunch break and 15-minute rest break in the morning and evening. When we got there the Jap guards turned us over to the dock bosses. Much the same way as they did it a Hirohata, we were divided up into, most of the time, our own squads and sent in different directions to do many different things. Two or three of the more feeble men were left at the office and attended the big kawa of soy bean that was put on to cook each morning for the Japanese as well as the prisoners. This alone made it worthwhile to work if you were able. The food in the camp for those on sick call, were half rations.

The first day our squad caught the job of moving 100 kilo sacks of soy beans from a barge anchored along the bank to railroad cars about 15 yard from the bank. Now 100 kilo bags weigh 220 pound in the good old USA. If someone had told me before I went down that morning that I would be lugging around 220 pounds of soy beans on my shoulders, I would have surely gone to that doctors office immediately. But here I was and there was that Jap boss with his stick, as usual, shouting "Kuda, Kuda, Sanyo, Sanyo" (Hurry, Hurry, Work, Work) Listening to them all day sounded like a broken record. I think those were the only two words they knew. He picked two big men, took them to the barge and showed them what he wanted. They got on each end of the bag of beans and together lifted it up about chest high as the Jap boss slipped under the bag, raised up and took off with the bag of beans, up a long heavy timber 12 inches wide by three inches thick and 20 foot long, laid between the edge of the railroad car and the ground. He dumped it in the corner of the car. We were standing there, mouths agape, not believing what we have just seen. He then grabbed a man by the arm and shoved him under the bag of beans the two men have lifted up and they put it on his back. The second the sack hit the man's shoulder, he collapsed with the bag of beans on top of him. The Jap started screaming and hitting the sack beside the man with the stick, then he reached down and pulled him up, shoved him aside and motioned for another man. Since I am standing there, the nearest, and I know he means me. I can just see me on the deck with a sack of beans on top of me, but I didn't hesitate for fear he might, this time, use that stick on me instead of the sack of beans. I tried to remember how he did it. I stepped up and, as the men lifted the beans, slipped under it and met it on the way up so that gravity didn't have a chance to accelerate the sack on the way down. I started off, but stumbled on another sack there on the deck, regained my balance and started up the plank. I could feel my knees start to buckle, but I kept going. All of a sudden, it felt like the plank was working with me as I put one foot down while the other foot is coming up, momentarily letting the plank come up and boost the other foot as it comes down. What you are doing is making the plank and gravity work with you instead of against you. I dumped the sack on the deck and the two men stacked it in place, then I returned down the plank while the Jap was yelling "Joto" Joto" at me. Meaning I did a good job. He is complimenting me. I went to the end of the line and another man tried it. He staggered up the plank, almost folding a couple of times, but he made it to the top. Then the Jap showed them again, trying to do it in slow motion and doing a good job of it. This went on for most of the morning. The second time I did it, I tried to remember what I did the first time. I shouldn't even think, as I almost did not make it that time. The third time I just walked up to it like I had been doing it forever. From then on, I just went by the feel and rhythm and tried not to think about it. Poor Pug, it took him forever to get the feel of it. Of course, as big as he was, he could do it just by main strength and awkwardness. It did not take Bill very long to be doing it the easy way, and by noon we were all improving. Before the day was over, with a belly full of soy beans at noon, we were not old hands but getting close.

I was so elated at realizing that I could carry a 220 pound sack of beans that I hadn't though much about my wound. It hadn't hurt any, or lets say I was not cognizant of it bothering me. When I got in that night, like all the other POWs, we hit the wash rack first. Even if we couldn't take a bath, we could pour enough water out of our canteen cup over our bodies to make a reasonable facsimile of it. While I was there I removed the strap and cover and washed out the gauze pad. The only difference I could see was the pad seemed to have absorbed a little more fluid from the wound.

This was the first time I had ever removed the dressing with anyone around. When I was in Hirohata, I would usually change the dressing before the workers came in to give them all the space they needed for their own cleanliness. So when I removed my shirt and pants and took off the pad, I had quite an audience. Pug was the first one to notice it. and blurted out, "God, Mate, how do you work with that hole in your side?" "You ought to be in a hospital. Then they all wanted to know all the details. Wanting to know if it was painful. To which I replied, "Not near as much as those poor guys with all the burn scabs. I would not trade with them any day." But, for some reason, from then on most of the guys in our squad seemed to marvel that I could go out each day and do as much as the best of them.

This happened one day when we were unloading 100 pound sacks of cement. We were carrying one bag at a time and believe you me that 100 pound sack of cement felt heavier than those 220 pound sacks of beans. We were trying to pick them up and put them on our shoulder to carry. That did you in fast. During morning break we were all a lot more fatigued than if we had been doing beans. Finally Bill Poulter, the assistant leader of our squad said he was going to ask the Jap boss if we couldn't do it like we did the beans. This was a different Jap and it was hard to get through to him, So Bill, Pug and I walk over to the cement pile and each one of them grabbed a corner of the sack and lifted it up and I walked under it and took off. The old Jap boss couldn't get over it. "Joto, Joto" (very good, very good,) "skoshi mati, Snayo" (small time, work) In other words that is very good, when break is up all men do it. So we set up two lines and emptied that car before quitting time. Pug asked if we could swim in the river. We had seen some Japanese women workers swimming up river a few days before. The Jap look at his watch, looked a us with a big smile and said very emphatically "OK, Joe".

It did not take him long to find a good spot to swim. We just wished we had clean clothes to put back on. That did not stop most of us from hitting the water. It was nice. Not too cold and not too hot. While we were making like a bunch of teenagers in a swimming pool, several Japanese women came down the path that ran along the bank of the river. When they saw us they stopped in their tracks and started giggling and chatting among themselves like a bunch of magpies. They would point and then giggle some more. The old Jap honcho was having as much fun as the women. We finally decided that we could not stay submerged forever and started resuming our soaping up and washing off. And the women giggled some more. Finally the Jap Honcho yelled out at them and waved them to be on their way. Then turned to us and made some statement no one could understand and started laughing. Finally he waved to us to come in and get dressed and "housue kiru" (house come back) In other words time to go to the camp.

The Jap are real shrewd. That Jap figured if we could empty two cars in one day and still have time to take a swim in the river, we could maybe empty three cars. Now we had not been behind the door while we had been working for them and talked about it on the way to the camp. Pug said we were going to have to play it cool and take easy so we could just do 2 cars the next day. We were not going bust our gut just to take a dip in the river. So when we went in the next morning, sure enough that Jap let it be known that he expected us to do three cars and then go swimming. Was he ever surprised. we stayed busy, working two lines, but taking a little longer to carry the sack of cement from the car to the place where they were being stacked. By noon we had just about finished the first car. Just before we went back to work The Jap honcho let it be know that he was not happy with the situation. We knew he was trying for the three car so he would get a pat on the back from the big Honcho. He told Pug if we did not finish the second car and start on the third we could not swim in the river and would have to work longer

Pug turned to us and told us what the deal was. One of the Turks piped up with I can carry two sacks at a time and if we all carry two sacks we can still go swimming. Pug gave him a go to hell look and told him to keep his ideas to himself. But first off this Turk walks up and says put two on. The guys lifting the sacks looked at Pug and he nodded. When he came back the second time, Pug ask him if he would like to carry three sacks. The Turk smarted off and that he could carry four. He was a well built as if he had lifted weights some time in his lifetime. Pug nodded to the lifter to load 4 on him. He got about half way back to the stack and started screaming dropping the sacks and clutching his right groin. Two of his countrymen rushed to him, picking him up as the Jap honcho started yelling, "Kuds, Kuda, Sanyo, Sanyo" swing his stick in the air as if to find someone to land on. Everyone went back to work. The Jap honcho went over to check on the Turk who was still moaning and clutching his groin. Shortly the Turk and his two pals, left with him, supported between the other two. We went back to work and emptied the car about 5 minutes before quitting time. The old Jap honcho was not happy and grumbled to himself all the way back to office where the other squads were waiting to go back to camp. We were told the Turk had been carried back to camp on a cart pulled by his two pals, escorted by an unhappy army guard who had been awakened from an afternoon snooze.

On the way back in, I ask Pug what he thought happened to him. He told he knew what had happened. "I've been having trouble with that smart ass for over a year. He is a show off and always trying to make every one think he is the hot stuff. He just makes it harder on everyone he works with. Always showing off and then the Jap Honchos expect all the other men to measure up to what he does. I also know that he has a hernia in his right groin. A couple of time in the past the hernia has become strangulated. The blood rushes in and closes the opening in the abdomen and causes excruciating pain. I hated to do it and was not sure it would strangulate if he over loaded. But it did and hopefully that cunt will get the point. I had heard of strangulation when I had a hernia in my younger years. But I had outgrown mine and was to be haunted later on in life by such a hernia in the same spot from lifting too much on the job.

When his pals got him into camp the doctor started putting cold towels on the area to reduce the swelling. He was still in pain and moaning when we went to bed that night and by morning was much better. So much so that the Jap guard was going to sent him out. The doctor explained the situation to the Jap and he got a days rest in camp. on half rations. Needless to say he did not try to show off any more after that. As I told Pug later, "That sure is a hell of a way to learn a lesson". he just said, Some men have to learn the hard way. You just can't tell them anything. I honestly think Old Pug sort of regretted doing what he did. But it was for the good of the whole camp. It takes an special kind of man to make those type of decisions. That is the reason they are leader, sergeants, officers etc. Pug Barron was that type man.

On one day, the Honchos divided our squad into three units and directed us in three directions. Pug and Bill took two of the squads, putting me in charge of the third group, which consisted of the Australians and the Greeks and three or four Limeys. we were sent across the river on a barge to a big warehouse where they were loading bales of dried fish into boxcars. When we arrived the Honcho indicated to me that the switch engine had not brought the cars in yet, then pointed to a stack of boxes and told us to stay there and wait. With that he took off to find out why the boxcars were not there. As usual each nationality went to their separate spot. Being the only American in the bunch. I ambled over to where the Australians were and listen in on their conversations. I had spoke to all of them at one time or another and they responded, but not all that enthusiastically. Today was no different. Finally one tall lanky guy with a weather beaten face, remarked when our eyes chanced to meet "What's your rank, Mate?" When I told him I was a buck sergeant, he said, "Me too." Then he wanted to know what state I was from. I told him I was from Texas. That must have broken the ice. They all had a good

I Was There, Charley

laugh and made some Texan jokes and next thing I knew we were talking like long lost brothers. I don't know why, but every time you tell someone foreign to you that you are from Texas, you always get a laugh. The best remark one of them made was, "If they had to have a boss, they couldn't do much better than a sergeant from Texas, instead of a Limey." After that I got along fine with them. The Jap started dividing the groups as work started falling off due to the fact that no ships were coming in to be unloaded. Which meant they had to find work for small groups, not large ones. So I was thrown with them more often.

The tall lanky one was named, Charles Graham. They all called him old Charlie. He was the oldest of the group and seemed to be their leader and advisor. He and four others had a big sheep ranch in the outback north of Perth, Australia, and gave his address as North Perth, West Australia. They all had decided they should do their duty for their country, so they drew straws or something on that order to see who would go and who would stay and take care of the sheep ranch. So three of them volunteered and ended up in Java after being shipped around over the South Pacific. Of the three, two of them still remained. One died in their only short combat, the other one got separated but the last he heard was still alive. They were all just regular guys, definitely clannish but I found out if they liked you, you were one of them. They couldn't understand my associations with Pug and Bill. But supposed they were a little prejudiced against the British as a whole.

I did not get that feeling from Pug or Bill about the Aussies. They never, to my knowledge, ever said any thing bad about Australians. But I guess that comes from being professional soldiers. Both Pug and Bill were married and had families, all grown. They were both in their 50s. and not far out of retirement. When things started heating up in the orient with the Japanese on the rampage across Manchuria and then into China, it was inevitable that something would sooner or later have to give and they would be engaged in combat. They sent their wives home about a year before war broke out. Their service had always been in the China-India-Burma area. So it had been close to 5 years since they had seen their family. But as Bill says, "That's the lot of a professional soldier. You learn to live with it or get out."

Air Raid warnings were a daily thing shortly after we had arrived at Fusiki. During these times of the warnings we were more or less left to our own devices. As soon as the first blast of that siren, the Jap honchos did a disappearing act. In other words, heading for the nearest bomb shelter they had dug up and down the river and dock. When this happened we just took a good long rest break, sat and rested until the all clear siren was blown. This might be on a barge load of beans, or in a cement warehouse and most any place where we were working. Often, if outside on and unloading detail, we would lay back on the sacks of beans and watch the bombers fly by, so high that you knew this was not their target. They were after more strategic targets. But not long before the end, Navy dive-bombers started working over the smaller ports.

On one such night the air raid sirens went off sometime after we had gone to bed. We could hear airplane motors and seemingly close by so we all rushed outside and not a camp guard was in sight. As we looked up, some 15 U.S. Navy bombers came roaring over our camp flying so low we could see the pilots silhouetted in their cockpits. Not less that 15 or 20 seconds later we heard loud explosions and fire filled the sky further down the coast from our camp. This went on for some 30 minutes as they came out of a dive, circling over our camp and heading back to make another run. I never found out what they hit unless it was another little port down the way. That thought sort of got us all to thinking about the possibility of them hitting Fusiki. If they hit at night we had nothing to worry about, for our camp was a good mile from the port area, but if they should try it in the daytime, we would be right in the middle of it all. Fortunately, we never saw any more Navy planes until they came over dropping food stuff to us after the surrender.

Bombers did come over the Fusiki one night and the sirens went off, but we did not see anything, just made out the dull throb of a high-flying motor. The next morning when we went to work, I caught the beans unloading detail. We were sitting on the boxcar waiting for the tug to bring a barge load of beans from the ship out in the middle of the channel. The tug was a little small narrow boat that literally tugged the barge from a long tow line that was strung out 50 or 75 feet behind, powered by a small one cycle gasoline engine that putt-putted along. As the tug neared the shore where he was to drag the barge, there was a loud explosion like a 500 lb bomb hit and exploded. Where the barge had been was nothing but empty space and suddenly it was raining water and beans. We were thoroughly soaked, and beans almost completely covered the ground around us. Of course when this happened the Honchos took off for their foxholes. The Tugboat was going around in circles. I think the concussion must have knocked the operator out for a little while. Finally the tug straightened out and we could see the driver back at the wheel heading for the other side of the channel. It must have been 15 or 20 minutes before the honchos showed up again. The first thing that crossed our mind was if we had to wait for another barge to be loaded, we would not have enough time to cook a pot of beans for lunch. Then, since the ground was covered with beans, we started picking them up where they had fallen on the concrete pier. By the time the Honchos came back we had enough beans in that pot for lunch. The Honchos took a dim view of it at first, but after taking a second thought, told the two men who usually tended the beans to build their fire. They washed the beans before they were cooked to remove any debris that might have found its way into the pot.

The big boss came out of the office and had a session with the others, who in turn told Pug that we would just have to wait for another barge to be loaded. They told Pug during the air raid warning a bomber the night before must have flown over and dropped harbor mines and one landed in the channel instead of in the outer harbor. Later in the morning, the Jap navy had a sweeper out in the harbor and several loud explosions were heard.. That was the nearest we came to being bombed while POWs. We often wondered how the tug missed the mine and the barge didn't. But the on second thought, the tug was so narrow it missed the mine and the barge being so much wider, a corner hit it and that was all she wrote. I bet that tug operator was thanking his lucky stars that whoever was watching over him decided it wasn't yet his time. An hour or so later another barge was brought over and an hour later it was lunchtime.

Right after lunch the air raid sirens went off again and for another 15 or 20 minutes we sat and waited for the honchos to come back. We usually unloaded two barges a day, but we did good that day to get the one unloaded. The honchos were not happy and growled at us all day. I guess had I been in their shoes, I would probably be watching the skies too and not been on my best behavior.

About three weeks after we had been at Fusiki, I had taken the tube out of my back. It did not seem to be draining so I imagined it might be healing. I was still a little bit leery, remembering what had happened before in Hirohata and Capt Seid had to lance it again. I was getting a little antsy about it, but not feeling any worse. A couple of weeks later my ears started ringing and I knew I must be running a little fever. So I told Pug I was going to stay in camp a day and see what happened. I was not feeling all that well anyway. After everyone had gone. I climbed back in my bunk and slept most of the day, my ears ringing worse now. I got my half ration and supplemented it with a small can of some sort of fish we had stolen out of a warehouse. In fact we had a whole case and divided it among the squad. That night I woke up and felt something moist under my right hip. In my fevered state, I thought I might have wet my bunk, but upon further examination it felt gooey. Then I noted my ears were not ringing as badly and I was feeling much better. I had kept wearing the pad because, although the hole had healed up, it was still tender to the touch

It was a good thing I'd kept wearing the pad, because it was soaked. Then I knew what had happened. Although the incision had healed, the two weeks drainage had built up enough pressure to force it open again. I eased out of the bunk with my blankets and made my way to the wash rack, cleaned myself, replaced the soiled pad with a clean one, examined the blanket and figured it could wait till morning to be cleaned up, then went back to bed.

The next morning the camp was all abuzz. One of the men who had been at Kobe and badly burned died during the night. One of the corps men told the British WO1 the man evidently had suffered lung damage in the fire and died of pneumonia. I had decided I would stay in camp another day to wash blankets and pads and see

I Was There, Charley

how it went before going back to work again. Right after the noon meal I had gone back to my bunk, when the British Commander came in and wanted to know if I could help prepare the dead man for cremation. I told him that I had helped in a couple of funerals at Hirohata, then went into detail of what had to be done, about the barrel and all. He asked the Jap commander, but he refused to listen, as much as saying he would get the urn but that was all he would do. He did assign a Jap guard to help us. The Jap guard left and came back with a two-wheel cart. It had a rod in the shape of a "T" extending from the axle of the two front wheels. A man got on each side of the rod and with the aid of the bar at the end of the rod, pulled the cart along. We went to the Jap garrison and loaded it with boards, sticks, beams. tree limbs and anything that would burn and brought it back to the camp. Then the guard made his way about 100 yards from the camp, in the middle of a rice paddy, with us bringing up the rear cart load of lumber. He then laid two big heavy timber 8 inches square three feet long about 6 feet apart, then proceeded to put the small stuff in between the two timbers. He took long pieces of flat boards and laid them on the timbers to form a bed of sorts. With that, he directed us to unload the cart and we returned to the camp

The body had been put in the so-called jail and stripped of all clothing. The four of us lifted the body, carried it out and put it on the cart The WO1 wanted to put something around it, but the Jap would not have that., so we carted him out to the funeral pyre, laid him on the planks that the Jap Guard had laid down and covered the body with the remainder of the lumber we had brought from the garrison. While we were placing the wood on the body, the Jap went to the camp and returned with what looked like a gallon can. When we finished placing all the lumber on the body, the Jap guard proceeded to pour the contents of the can on the pile of wood and then pitched a match on it. It immediately exploded into a massive fireball. We had to get fifteen or twenty feet away to keep the heat from baking us.

We watched for a few minutes and were then ordered to return to the camp. The Jap dismissed all but two of us, who returned the cart to the garrison. We were encircled by a 10-foot fence, so could not see how the fire was going, but could see the smoke from the fire rising above the fence most of the afternoon. After the men came in from work that afternoon, the WO1 commander went with the Japanese officer left on duty and retrieved some ashes for the urn and that night a funeral service was conducted by one of the Dutch POWs who served as Chaplain for his group. He conducted the services in both Dutch and English. This was the only death in Fusiki. I will have to say, by and large, this camp populace came out in better shape than when they went in.

I really never got to see too much of the camp until we were told the war was over. I think we were given two and maybe three rest days all the time we were there. They said they were going to give us one day rest out of twenty we worked. And I think that was pretty close to what we received. So if you were working every day, the time spent in camp was taken up with sleeping and washing clothes. That was the first thing we did when we came in. We headed to the wash rack and removed our clothes, washed our bodies, then our clothes and hung them on the rafters in the barracks to dry. By that time its chow down. After eating there was a little chit-chat, but it wasn't long before we were stretched out on our bunks, dead tired and ready for sleep.

The camp was situated on the rail line that ran out of the Fusiki dock area. Freight trains were in and out every day. Somewhere down the line, it must have split and one half going across a bridge over the river to the other side. Some of us, on numerous occasions had worked dock area on the other side, and there where rail lines on that side. The one occasion I had, to work that side of the dock area, about 75 of us were loaded on a barge and tugged over to that side. We were taken to a large warehouse in put to work rolling 55 gallon drum of some sort of liquid, probably a petroleum product, by the smell. We had to turn them on their side and them roll them down the dock, close to a block long, then up a wooden ramp in to a boxcar. Then sit them up on their end again. I was scared they would want us to stack them, but this was our lucky day. Then after thinking about it, that would not have been feasible.

Everything went along fine as long as we kept the barrel moving. But if you stopped to take a breather, one of those slant-eyed honchos was on your case, screaming and threatening you with their ever-present sticks. This was not like loading sacks of beans, where you got a little rest while in line waiting your turn to get the next sack. And would you know there were no air raid sirens to conveniently interrupt our labors this morning. On top of that, we were forced to work past our break time to finish filling up a car. When break time came, it was cut short because two honchos couldn't decide which one of their watches were right. Finally, the noon whistle blew, but we were kept at the job until all the barrels were moved out of the warehouse.

Pug and I slammed the door shut on the boxcar and climbed back on the dock, hoping to finally get a bite to eat in the shade of the warehouse. The honcho had a different idea. They marched us back to a little shack where they had their lunch stashed and let us out in the sun with no place to sit and nothing to sit on but the ground. That is when old Pug motioned for us to move to the shade of a warehouse about 50 ft away. Old slant eyes came roaring out of the shack yelling his head off and we kept moving toward the shade. About that time the air raid siren let out a chilling blast and that was the last we saw of those two nips for the next hour. They let their lunch where they were eating and completely disappeared. In fact, there was not a Jap in sight anywhere. The only bad thing about it was we missed out on the bowl of soybeans we were used to getting each day. At least we had a quiet hour or more before the all clear siren blew. Then the honchos came back and finished their lunch before we were put back to work.

This time they split the squad up and went off in two different directions. I went with Bill and our group went back to the other side of the dock to load out a boxcar of cardboard boxes of what turned out to be small cans of what I would call sardines. The boxes did not have any labels on them, so the only way we could find out what was in them was to accidentally drop one. Of course this brought down the wrath of the honcho, who we noticed later was stuffing cans of the fish in his shirt. He could not be everywhere all the time, so many boxes of fish did not get to its destination filled to the brim, so to speak. Once we got in the car, the top of a case was ripped opened and we stuffed cans in our shirts. We would then close the flaps and cover the box with one that had not been opened. That went on all afternoon until the car was loaded.

A couple of the men had to take a benzyo (toilet) break which was out behind the warehouse and while they were gone they found a culvert that ran under the rail line and we handed down several boxes of fish and they shoved them in the culvert for future retrieval. The culvert was only a short distance from the shack were we reported in each morning, making it easy to go to the benzyo and at the same time, retrieve a few cans of fish. I think we still had fish stashed away when we surrendered.

We finished the car out before regular quitting time and went on back to the check-in shack. There was still beans in the pot, so we proceeded to fill our mess kits with beans and carried them in to camp and gave them to some of the sickly men who were on half rations. I think if we had not brought in food to give them, some of them would not made it out of that camp. We were most fortunate in Fusiki in that the Jap guards did not hold their shakedowns like they did at Hirohata. In fact, once the guards had us inside the gate, we did not see much of them after that. They did not cruise through the barracks looking for trouble. The British WO1 pretty much ran the camp inside.

One light side occurred while we were working this dock area. Every morning shortly after we arrived at the shack and while waiting to be assigned our daily tasks, this little Japanese girl among others who worked in the offices in the dock area would pass by the staging area. This one girl was younger than the others and we would whistle at her. The Jap guards didn't seem to object and she seemed to like it, as she always gave us a shy smile. She always seemed to have no friends as she was always by herself. It got to be a ritual, she passed by and we whistled but we never saw her in the afternoon. On his particular afternoon we had got through early and were hanging around the shack waiting for the other groups to come in. Charlie (my Australian buddy) and I decided we would go to the

I Was There, Charley

benzyo and get a few cans of fish before we went in. While we were busy getting the box out of the culvert, our girl-friend came by and caught us red-handed. What to do? I said "Konnitiwa" (good day). and offered her a couple of cans of fish, holding my forefinger to my lips. She looked startled for a moment and then looked all around, nodded her head, took the cans and stuffed them in a bag she was carrying, smiled sweetly and walked on. We loaded up, expecting that to be the last day we would have the chance, not knowing what the little girl would do.

We let it ride for a few days and then went back to taking a few cans in to the half-ration folks. We would see her in the morning and get the usual smile. A week of so later, while we were waiting for the Jap guards to come down and get us, we saw her coming and, not seeing any honchos around, made like we were going to the benzyo and when she got closer, motioned her over and pointed at the culvert. She smiled and nodded, so we gave her some more fish. This time, very softly, she muttered the word "arigrato" (thank you) and hurried on her way. She started coming by regularly every afternoon. One afternoon, Charlie motioned to the soy bean pot. She gave him a big smile and took out a small "bento box" (lunch box), handed it to him and he filled it up. While she was putting it back in her bag, the Honcho came out of the shack and wanted to see what she had in the box. I was holding my breath for fear he would look in the bag and find the fish. But when she showed him the soy beans, his only remark was "joto" and then said something else to her in Japanese, then turned and went back in the shack. She turned to Charlie and the rest of us, bowed politely, smiled that shy smile and hurried off to her home. I guess the Japs were beginning to, after daily air raids, see the end and decided to be agreeable. After that, she got her daily ration of soy beans and a can or two fish if she showed up. I don't know, but I imagine she did not have any set hours and came and went as her job demanded.

Another day, toward the end of July or the first part of August 1945, we were put to doing work that was not stevedore type labor. The ships were getting further and further in their arrivals. Thus, there were days when it seemed they had to manufacture work for us to do. This one day was a 'Lulu.' They had built forms out past the loading dock, probably planning on extending it on further out. The gravels had been hauled in on a rail car and dumped at the edge of the railroad. The cement mixer was drug in by a bull cart and set up by the gravel pile. Here they were mixing the cement and we were carrying it to the forms some 75 yards away.

The set up a crew of men hauling water in barrels, and another group carrying sacks of cement from the warehouse and another group carrying the finished concrete in hods on their shoulder to the forms. I got caught in the hod-carrying detail. We would back up to the cement mixer, set down on a rail while the operator tilted the mixer drum and let the wet concrete pour in the hod. (probably 100 to 150 pounds), then take off up a ramp to the top of the dock and walk the 75 yards to the place where they were pouring the forms. There was a ramp constructed of planks around the forms on which to walk. When you got to the position, you backed up to the forms and a Jap pulled a lever and the bottom of the hod dropped out, pouring cement into the forms.

They were working one mixer to start with, but decided there was too much time wasted waiting in line to get your hod filled. During the morning break they brought around another mixer and things picked up. Everyone had to work harder. The water carriers had to make more trips. The cement carriers had to carry twice as many sack of cement, so by the time we hod carriers made a round trip we didn't get to stand in line and wait, but load up and make another trip. Believe you me that was one long day. I found out by the end of the day that they were extending the dock on out and were going to enlarge the warehouse. But they were going to have to wait a day for the cement to set up. Then they were going to haul in a carload of sand to fill in the formed in area and then pour a concrete slab over it. We were doing the labor, hauling all that sand the 75 yards to fill that hole. That was more than one carload of sand. I don't know if that dock was ever was finished. Three days later Japan surrendered. I could have cared less.

On the morning of August 15, 1945 it was up and at 'em as usual. We made the trip to the dock area. We sat around waiting for them to make up their minds what they were going to do and where we were going. Honchos came and went, constantly yelling out one of their names and saying "denwa" (telephone). The guys that were cooking the beans for the day were busy getting their fire started and beans and water in the pot. As the hands on the old clock on the shack wall approached 9:00 a.m., we were sitting around waiting for something to happen. We could see the coolies on the one little old island boat unloading something into a barge at the side. There was a string of flat cars on the siding along the dock. We figured some of us would be unloading the barge onto the rail cars. Finally along toward 10:00 a.m. one of the honchos came out and called Pug over and I heard him say, "Kio, Yasume, Asti, sanyo" (today, rest, tomorrow, work). Pug then turned and told us to fall in, we were going back to camp. So, without any Jap guards we headed for the camp.

Here we found the camp all abuzz with the rumor that the war was over. The Jap in charge of the kitchen was supposed to have told the cooks that Japan had surrendered, but so far no official notice from the commander. We lay around all day with the Japanese coming and going and even some new faces we had not seen. The cooks said extra rations had been issued so we would have a larger evening meal. Of course we, who had gone to work, just ate our mess kit of rice for the noon meal. Those who stayed in camp made do on what we had been able to bring in to them. I managed to wash up all my clothes and pads and get then dry. In case we had to go to work the next day.

After a quiet night, I woke up to a lot of chatter that was different from the usual morning rituals. Someone said that the Jap guards were all gone. Then a loud whistle summoned us out to the courtyard for morning count down. But instead of a count down, the WO1 announced that it was not official, but the war was over. The commandant had gone and all the guards with him. No one was there except the Japanese civilian who had been acting as interpreter, who was to make an announcement in a few minutes. Shortly the little Interpreter came out of the office and read from a piece of paper he had in his hand. Japan had surrendered. He had been ordered to tell us to remain in our camps and Allied officials would be making the necessary arrangements for our release. We were to paint large P.W.s on the roof of our barracks. He pointed to four buckets of paint and brushes he had arranged for that purpose. There was plenty of food in the storeroom. With that he bid us "God Speed" and left.

Departing Fusiki POW Camp, Sept 1945

CHAPTER SEVEN
WE ARE GOING HOME SEPT, 5--30, 1945

The British WO1 assumed command and asked all non-commissioned officers to stay awhile, then dismissed the others for breakfast as soon as it was prepared. He appointed a leader for each of the American, British, Dutch and Australians groups, and the other nationalities formed another group, with an older, respected Hindu they called 'Chiefy,' as their designated leader. He said we were going to operate this camp just like any military installation. We were to organize our respective groups as they were before we became POWs. The Americans had a shortage of non-commissioned officers, or non-com's. In fact, we had to dig deep to find enough bodies to fill the non-com slots. We had one Staff Sergeant who agreed to be the top dog. Many of the Americans had been in the fire at Kobe and were not able to do even the lightest of chores. As it turned out, we were able to find sixteen Corporals to take the sixteen squads of eight. We were so short of men, some of the squads did not even have eight. There were only 138 Americans in the camp, but we set it up like an infantry company, four squads to a platoon and four platoons in a company, with a sergeant in charge of each platoon and the Staff Sergeant in charge of the battery. This is the way we organized our group and the other groups had similar type organizations.

The main object of all this was to get a name, rank and serial number of each man and the outfit to which he belonged, so we would have something to report when we were released. As it turned out, the only thing they really wanted was the number and nationality. But the organization did aid the WO1 in determining duties to be performed and delegating their performance, sort of a chain-of-command which proved helpful during the next twenty days we were there; if for no other reason than to get all of us into some semblance of a military organization. As it turned out, this WO1 was a spit and polish commander and had us all towing the line and assuming the epitome of decorum.

We had morning muster in the courtyard daily, with each squad leader reporting the condition of his squad, those sick and unable to make muster, to the platoon commander and the platoon commander reporting the same to the Commandant. This way we could keep up with every man in the camp, not that they were going anywhere. We had police call, where a line is formed and moved across the compound, picking up any trash that might be around. Each platoon was assigned the task of keeping their section of the camp clean and halfway decent, considering what we had to work with. There were plenty of hands to do the job, since we had close to 300 men. In fact, there was a lot of leisure time. We had 24-hour guard duty, with a very formal change of the guard every afternoon at 6:00. A lot of the men griped about the spit and polish, but deep down I think, from my own experience, it was good to get back to doing something on my own instead of having a club held over my head day in and day out.

After our first non-coms meeting, many suggestions were made for improving the food situation. We had plenty of rice, but nothing to go with it. We started missing the old stand-by 'greens soup.' All of us who had been working knew where there was plenty of food to be had…in the warehouse area. We saw bull carts go by the camp every day. So all we had to do was commandeer one of them, take it to the dock area and get what we wanted, but the Commandant reflected his professionalism. He announced that just because the allies had defeated Japan, this was no reason we should take advantage of their people   He suggested we make up some sort of 'promise to pay' voucher and he would sign it   Later, they could present it to the occupation officials for recompense. Then one sergeant mentioned that we would have to put a fair price on the articles or service we paid, or the Japanese could just go to the occupation officials and name any price they wanted. After bouncing it around for most of the afternoon, we arrived at what we considered a workable method of obtaining food and services fairly.

So we cornered the first bull cart that came down the road and, as we had some POWs who, in three and half years, had learned the language good enough to dicker with the Japanese and we soon had the use of a bull cart. The only drawback was we had to let the Jap do the driving, as the bull would not respond to our commands. That was no problem because there was a market not far from the camp, where we could get some fruit and vegetables. After we made the rounds of the dock area and brought enough canned goods to last awhile, we made another trip and a different group of POWs was sent to the market. The hang-up here was they arrived late in the afternoon and the picking was pretty slim; however, they managed to get enough greens and turnips for the next days lunch. Later trips proved more fruitful, in spite of the fact that fruit was very scarce. We had no trouble with the Japanese taking the chits. Later, when the officials found our camp, a report was given them of what we had done and so far as I know, it was acceptable. As to whether the people were reimbursed, I have no way of knowing. After the B-29s started dropping food on the camp, we did not need the old Jap and his bull cart any longer, but he came by every day just in case.

After three day of not seeing any action in the sky, we thought maybe the camp was so new there was no record of our being here. Just because we could see the bombers flying overhead did not mean they could see us, even though I knew we would be found eventually. Until we started making our visit to the market and the dock area, we did not know there was another POW camp in the area, but on one of our visits to the market the men ran into some more allied POWs doing the same thing we were, and we found out there was another camp on the other side of the river. Later on, when the Air Corps got a notice of this other camp and flew a food drop over it, they saw the PW on our camp and reported it. That night I was Sergeant of the Guard. The Corporal on duty had to make a pit call to the benzyo and as I was awake, I filled in for him. He had no more than reached the 'john' when I heard: "Corporal of the Guard, Post number one," which meant he needed assistance or something was up. Post number one was the main gate. It was about 50 feet from the guardhouse. When I arrived at the gate, it was open and a U.S. Jeep was sitting there with its motor idling. I could make out two men in the front seat and one in the back. As I moved closer, I could see the eagle on the shoulder of the man sitting beside the driver. I walked up and saluted and gave him my name and rank. He saluted, dismounted and stuck out his hand for me to shake. Then he put his hand around my shoulder and told me it was good to see that I had not forgotten how to be a soldier, then asked to see the Commander. The Corporal had returned and saluted, so I sent him to awaken the WO1. I then turned back to the Colonel, telling him we were an international camp with a British Army WO1 as camp commander. He then wanted to know if there wasn't an officer in the camp. I told him about the doctor not wanting to take charge and suggesting the WO1. He did not seem to be unduly perturbed at the status quo and when the WO1 arrived, dismissed me and exchanged pleasantries with the commander.

I then went to the jeep and asked the other two men if they would like some tea, explaining it was all we had as coffee was not one of the Japanese popular drinks. The driver was a Sergeant and the other man was a First Lieutenant and the Colonel's Aide. They were all Air Corps. They accepted the tea and offered the Corporal and me the first American cigarette in three and half years. I had never smoked until I was taken prisoner, but the Jap almost always had a cigarette allowance. I would get mine and trade that for food. Later, as the food ration was cut even more, I started smoking to dull the hunger pangs. Most all the Red Cross boxes had cigarettes in them, but they were usually British or South African. I did get to smoke a Camel one time aboard an ore ship we were unloading. A Chinese cook gave it to me. So, for all practical purposes, I was a smoker but not of American cigarettes, and this was quite a come up in the world. Before he left, the driver went to his jeep and brought back two packs and gave them to the Corporal and me.

Japanese Cigarette Package

The Colonel and the Commander drank their tea and pow-wowed for a good hour. These goings on were at the ungodly hours of 1:00 and 2:00 in the morning. We had a change of guard at 2:00 and were still talking, consuming a lot of tea our own selves. The Lieutenant joined the Colonel and WO1 after awhile. All that tea got to the driver and he said he had to go to the 'john,' so the Corporal showed him the way. When he returned, he made the remark that we were a bit primitive, and then laughed about it. They finally left around 2:30 a.m. The WO1 jokingly offered them accommodations for the remainder of the night, but the Colonel said the Jeep looked pretty good to him.

After they left, the WO1 said they had had a good long talk. The Colonel told him all the news of the surrender and how they found out about our camp. Sure enough, the Japanese kept no record of our camp. He promised us a B-29 loaded with barrels of food within the next day or so. He was amazed that we were getting along so well as an international group. This news must have gotten out to the press, because after I got back to the states, a big article about our camp, with pictures, appeared in November 16, 1945 edition of 'Yank,' the Armed Services Magazine. He said it might be as long as two to three weeks before we could be moved out, the Japanese rail system being what it was. After all, the Japanese had to keep moving also or there would be chaos throughout the island.

The next morning after breakfast, while we were engaged in our many chores of keeping the place looking like a well-run army post, the roar of motors filled the air and Navy dive-bombers buzzed the camp, making two or three runs, dipping his wings and cavorting around. Finally, on a last run not more than a hundred feet in the air, he threw out a package, which landed in the middle of the courtyard. It was a note saying: "I am leaving now, but I'll be back with help." Given our proximity to the coastline, we figured he would be coming back pretty soon. But after the noon meal and no planes and mid-afternoon and no planes, we had about decided he had forgotten us or lost his way. But no…he was not going to disappoint us. Shortly after 4 p.m. we heard the sounds before we saw them, then they were on top of us. Six of them…flying in formation. They peeled off and came in low and started dumping packages. One after another until all six had made their run. Then dipping their wings, they left the way they came. We were too busy dodging packages to really know just how much fell and where. Many of the men opened the gate and went out to retrieve packages dropped in the rice fields adjoining the compound. Some of the packages broke open when they hit and spread food everywhere. It must have taken a good hour to locate it all. There was just about everything you could imagine in that drop. The canned goods were taken to the kitchen, the remainder, all brand names of candy. cookies, powdered milk, peanut butter snacks, you name it - we kept and divided with the men not able to participate in the food hunt.

I Was There, Charley

Picture of Air Corps Drop just as parachutes open

Clemens A. Kathman

レンゴウグンホリョヘ
ALLIED PRISONERS

The JAPANESE Government has surrendered. You will be evacuated by ALLIED NATIONS forces as soon as possible.

Until that time your present supplies will be augmented by air-drop of U.S. food, clothing and medicines. The first drop of these items will arrive within one (1) or two (2) hours.

Clothing will be dropped in standard packs for units of 50 or 500 men. Bundle markings, contents and allowances per man are as follows:

BUNDLE MARKINGS				BUNDLE MARKINGS			
50 MAN PACK	500 MAN PACK	CONTENTS	ALLOWANCES PER MAN	50 MAN PACK	500 MAN PACK	CONTENTS	ALLOWANCES PER MAN
A	3	Drawers	2	B	10	Laces, shoe	1
A	1-2	Undershirt	2	A	11	Kit, sewing	1
B	22	Socks (pr)	2	C	31	Soap, toilet	1
A	4-6	Shirt	1	C	4-6	Razor	1
A	7-9	Trousers	1	C	4-6	Blades, razor	10
C	23-30	Jacket, field	1	C	10	Brush, tooth	1
C	10	Belt, web, waist	1	B	31	Paste, tooth	1
A	11	Capt, H.B.T.	1	C	10	Comb	1
B	12-21	Shoes (pr)	1	B	32	Shaving cream	1
A	1-2	Handkerchiefs	3	C	12-21	Powder (insecticide)	1
C	32-34	Towel	1				

There will be instructions with the food and medicine for their use and distribution.

C A U T I O N

DO NOT OVEREAT OR OVERMEDICATE   FOLLOW DIRECTIONS

INSTRUCTIONS FOR FEEDING 100 MEN

To feed 100 men for the first three (3) days, the following blocks (individual bundles dropped) will be assembled:

3 Blocks No. 1
(Each Contains)

2 Cases, Soup, Can
1 Cases Fruit Juice
1 Case Accessory Pack

1 Block No. 5
(Each Contains)

1 Case Soup, Dehd
1 Case Veg Puree
1 Case Bouillon
1 Case Hosp Supplies
1 Case Vitamin Tablets

1 Block No. 3
(Each Contains)

1 Case Candy
1 Case Gum
1 Case Cigarettes
1 Case Matches

3 Blocks No. 2
(Each Contains)

3 Cases "C" Rations
1 Case Hosp Supplies
2 Cases Fruit

1 Block No. 7
(Each Contains)

1 Case Nescafe
1 Sack Sugar
1 Case Milk
1 Case Cocoa

1 Block No. 10
(Each Contains)

3 Cases Fruit
2 Cases Juice

List of food items in Air Corps Drop

Coming just before the evening meal, the cooks figured that, with all that junk food, they wouldn't be serving the usual amount,

I Was There, Charley

and they were right. I don't consider myself to be any smarter that anyone else, but when we got the first red cross boxes, a lot of the men stuffed themselves to the point some were really sick with diarrhea like they'd never had before, for the next few days. So I decided I was not going to indulge to the point of making myself sick. I ate my rice and vegetables, and soybeans like a good little boy. Then I slowly munched on a Hershey bar, hoping to sleep the night through. Such was not to be the case. Men were up vomiting, and running to the benzyo. I don't think anyone got much sleep that night. Only about half of the camp made morning muster. It was a quiet day around there, with a lot of moaning and groaning. I think most of them learned their lesson, and rightly so, because we hadn't seen the last of the food drops.

Two days later, so early in the morning we were barely up, we heard the drone of heavy bombers, B-29's, probably flying at a thousand feet. They went on over and we thought they were going somewhere. When almost out of sight, they turned around and approached much lower. One peeled away from the path toward us while the others kept coming. Then all of a sudden you could see the bomb bays opening up and barrels start falling out with colorful parachutes attached to slow their descent. What a sight. The sky was almost blacked out by the many parachutes falling. All in color. It was a beautiful sight. Once or twice I saw a barrel whose chute failed to open, shooting past the other parachutes and plowing into the ground, bursting and spewing its contents in every direction. The Colonel had warned us to stay in the building until all the chutes had fallen. As it was, one barrel must have been delayed in being kicked out, and fell on top of the back barracks. It went right through the tile roof into the top bay and through that to the ground. We didn't have to carry its contents far…the kitchen was right around the corner. If it rains now, anyone sleeping under that hole will get pretty damp.

After the drop was completed and all the barrels and scattered food was brought into camp, someone mentioned the second B-29 and where it had gone. We had been so busy observing the one flying our direction and the dropping of the food that the other B-

29 had been forgotten. Then some of the men remembered seeing fellow POWs in the vegetable market and by logical reasoning, it must have dumped its contents on that camp. We asked passing Japanese where the other camp in the area was. No one seemed to know, or else were not talking. Since we didn't venture far from the camp enclosure, there was not much chance of finding out anything. The other camp must have been wondering about us, and they were luckier than we were, and located our position. Their own camp commander and some of his men paid us a visit. They were on the other side of the river and up the coast from us. I don't remember if there was any mention of the type of work they had been doing.

Arrangements were made for both camps to take a day off and meet at the river for a get-together. There were quite a few men who met others they had soldiered with in their various units. I did not see anyone that I knew from the 200th CAC, but I ran into a couple from Texas, one from Lubbock. Since I attended to Texas Tech, we had something to talk about. I learned how lucky I was, the war ended when it did. If we had stayed there the coming winter, it would have been plenty rough. They said the winter before one blizzard banked up snow against the barracks a good 10 feet on one side and they shoveled their way out through the front of the buildings. Needless to say, they didn't go to work for a few days. They thought it would have been better if they had worked, so they would at least be moving around and keeping a little warm. As it was, they had to stay in their sack to keep reasonably comfortable. To top it off, the Jap put them on half rations until they went back to work.

We had a nice day and visit. Of course, the main topic of discussion was when we would be getting out of there. But at this point, what the heck, we had been waiting three and half years, another week wouldn't make a lot of difference. Our accommodations were not luxury suites, but the food was a big improvement. After what we had been through – with our stomachs satisfied, we excused a lot of other distractions. The fact we were free and not being harassed by a bunch of little egomaniac slant-eyes can make a lot of difference in your outlook on everything. We never had a chance to exchange pleasantries again and I not sure when they were moved out to their liberation point. Considering what they had gone through the past two or more years, they were happier to get out of there than we were.

All the time we had been at the Fusiki camp, we had known about the small army garrison down the road from our camp. It was here the guards came to take us to and from work. The garrison also provided the guards who were on duty at our camp 24 hours a day. We often saw one or two of them coming out of the house across the road from the camp, but it never occurred to us what they might be doing there. It was a rather large house by Japanese standards, set back from the street and surrounded by a lush growth of trees. The only time we had to observe anything was when we were going to or coming from the dock area. This roadway was lined with the typical small hovels, jammed closely together, so common in rural Japan at that time, with very small yards in front, neatly tended and distinctly different from the others. So the large house stood out in a distinctive way and marked it as something special.

And special it was, as we were soon to find out. One morning after being on guard duty the latter part of the night shift, I was making my rounds of the respective posts, which a Sergeant is required to do. I was talking to the man on guard at Post #1, the main gate, and opened it just to take a look at the sun rising and marvel at the beauty of a new day. I was so glad I was not trudging to the dock that morning, enjoying the sun coming up over that house across the street. It was such a beautiful morning, so quiet - birds chirping in the trees, a time of complete awareness, and this was the first time I had been able to thoroughly appreciate the beauty of a new day in the past three and half years. As he and I looked toward that house, we could barely make out the front porch, almost hidden in the shadows of the surrounding trees. Suddenly, the stillness was broken by a barrage of Japanese chatter as the door flew open and we saw two Japanese soldiers come out laughing, followed by two or three half dressed Japanese women, all obviously drunk. They fondled each other until they saw us watching, then the men took off rapidly down the road toward the garrison and the women stumbled over each other getting back in the house. Came the dawn. Now we knew we had a 'Japanese comfort house' across the street.

When the WO1 came in later that morning, I told him what I'd seen. At first he thought it was funny, but then immediately realized the dire consequents the situation might cause in the camp, and said so. We had 300 men in that camp who had not been with a woman in a long time. In spite of some of us being in bad physical condition, there were many, many more who were physically in pretty good shape from lugging 200 pounds sacks of beans around every day of the week, and he knew they would be over at the front door of the comfort house in the bat of an eye. He asked me to keep it under my hat and tell the other guard to do the same. But you know about gossip – it is impossible to keep it from spreading. The commandant ordered everyone out and tried, to the best of his ability to warn them of the consequences of visiting that place. By and large, the majority of the men did not need to be warned, but there are always those dare devil, know it alls who think it can't happen to them. The gate was open during the day with only a guard who had no authority to keep them from crossing the road. How many, I don't know, but I do know there was a lot of bragging going on that night and afterwards. Most of them must have forgotten the films we were shown when we were inducted into the service. Those films are horror films at best, and made a big impression on me, but I can't answer for others. My guess is that 14 to 21 days later there were a lot a sick calls with a diagnosis of gonorrhea and possibly syphilis. That kind of diagnosis can cost you a loss of rank, pay and a stretch in the guardhouse, to say nothing of the possibility of losing you life. But stupid is stupid.

After what seemed like an eternity, (it was three weeks) a train backed in one morning and we were ordered to board. We were going home. It did not take us long to pack what little we had, and be ready. Some photographers were on hand, and several reporters. The November issue of "Yank" newspaper came out with picture of our camp. What little I had, I acquired after we were told the war was over. The parachute the air corps used to drop the food was of bright colored nylon. I guess we all had the same idea, that material would make some nice, loud shirts. We tore them up and divided them among ourselves so we could all get different colors. I got some red, yellow and blue, which I gave to my two sisters and they sewed blouses out of it. Beside the chutes, I had my mess kit, cup, spoon, mirror, three little notebooks and my diary. A Japanese lady at a stop somewhere along the way, gave a bunch of us Japanese fans, and I still have mine. The mess kit and cup disappeared somewhere. The remainder, I still have. The diary and little books have been a great aid in compiling this book.

Most of the day into mid-afternoon, we passed through different stations where large crowds waited to catch trains. We saw many officers in uniform lose their swords to ex-POWs who got off the train and demanded them. I was surprised that the officers parted with their swords without some resistance. There were innumerable enlisted personnel in the crowded station platforms, but I did not see anything they had that I wanted. I believe if there had been anyone of them that had mistreated me I would maybe have done something about it, but probably not…I was so overjoyed at the thought of getting out of that place. It would have taken a lot to make me angry. It was a long day, and full of anticipation. Throughout the trip, we did not have a bite to eat, but who was noticing. The feeling of exuberance abounded in the cars as we made our way toward deliverance. If alcohol had been flowing freely in all those cars, which is wasn't, we could not have been more intoxicated. Tall tales were told and retold, stories of home and all its splendors, food we were going to eat, milk we were going to drink and drunks that would last for days. All were words of imagination and dreams of a starved mind and body.

When the train finally stopped and we looked out the window, we beheld the most beautiful sight. A whole bay full of U.S. Navy ships…every size and description. Every way you looked, as far as you could see, were ships and more ships, all anchored several hundred yards from the shore. As we detrained, Navy personnel directed us to smaller craft (LCMs) lined up along the shore with their ramps down so we could just walk right off the shore into the craft. As soon as the LCM was loaded, the ramp was raised and off we went, where too and which one we didn't know, there were so many ships out there. Not to worry…we soon recognized the big red cross on the Navy Hospital ship 'Rescue' anchored in the middle of the bay.

A ladder was suspended from the side of the ship, which we climbed to get to the deck. Here we were met with navy personnel who handed us a numbered basket for our personal belongings. This may be where I lost my mess kit and cup. A metal was hung around our necks, and it had the same number as our basket. Then we were shoved into an entranceway and told to disrobe. These guys wore rubber gloves and a mask, looking as if they were afraid of catching something from us. We tossed our clothes into a shoot which we were told (jokingly) would be used to fire the boilers, then we were directed to the showers of, guess what? Warm water. My first warm shower since leaving Angel Island and the good old USA back in September of 1941.

After the bath, we were air dried and dusted with DDT, then issued a pair of navy shorts and T-shirt, then we were paraded through a group of doctors who examined us…ears, nose, eyes and throat…took our temperature, pulse, and blood pressure and then lungs and heart. The last doctor looked at our feet, joints and body. When he came to the incision in my side with the rubber drain hanging out, the movement of the line came to a screeching halt. The doctor swallowed a couple of times and asked how long I had been in this condition. I told a little over a year. He swallowed again. "What happened?" he asked, so I told him the whole story. He shook his head. "I wouldn't believe it, if hadn't seen it," he said as he wrote something on a pad, tore it out and told me to give it to the corpsman at the door as I went to pick up my personal belongings. Then he said he would see me later.

From there I finished going through the line to get the remainder of my clothes issued. As I went out the door, picking up my belonging and turning in my tag, I handed the note to the corpsman He took one look at it and called another guy over and told him to take me below. This is when I found out the size of this Hospital ship. We must have walked a mile (slight exaggeration), finally coming to large double swinging doors and into a large wardroom with double bunks everywhere. He handed the note to a nurse, who was the first white woman I had seen in four years. Boy, Oh Boy - was she pretty and nice. She took me into her office and made out an admittance sheet, then asked to see the incision. I pulled my T-shirt up and lowered my waistband so she could see. Man, I thought she would fall out of that chair. "When was the last time this was dressed?" she asked. I told her I'd sterilized the tube and put on a new pad just this morning. She didn't seem impressed, and made me throw away the pad I'd just put on when I showered a short time ago. She 'clucked' her tongue a couple of times and led me to another room filled with all sorts of medicinal things, proceeded to rinse my side with alcohol, tape a bandage over it and said, "That will hold you until the doctor can see you."

We went back to her office and finished filling out my life history. We talked for a long time about prison camp. She said I was the first POW she had met. Then it dawned on her that she had better notify the galley that there would be a patient in that ward tonight. After that, we had another long session until my dinner came. It was about time. It was the first bite since early that morning. I did not realize how hungry I was until I smelled the food…a big steak still sizzling, hot French fries, hot bun, butter and green beans, with apple pie for dessert. The nurse asked what I wanted to drink. She had just made a fresh pot of coffee. COFFEE!! What is that? I can't believe I am hearing right. Do I want coffee? Does a hog want slop? I was just about to think I had died and gone to heaven.

I am not sure, but I think I almost ate plate and all. After finishing, I went into the nurse's office to get another cup of coffee. The day nurse was just going off and a new nurse was coming on. I was hitting the jackpot. Two pretty, white women in one day…almost more than this old soldier boy could stand. The new one was just as pretty and just as nice. We had a short chat while she was doing her bookkeeping for the nightshift. "Looks like you are going to have the ward to yourself tonight," she said. The doctor will see you tomorrow morning, he has been checking POW's in all day." She said all the able-bodied POWs were put aboard other ships going to Manila for processing. I asked her about the burned POWs that were in such bad shape at the camp. She said they were in quarantine or intensive care in another part of the ship, but because of my good physical condition and because the doctor wanted to see me personally, they had sent me to this ward, which was an ambulatory ward where patients are sent before retuning to duty or going home.

When she wasn't running errands, this nurse and I played 'Gin' until 10:00 p.m. I picked a bunk out of the many available, and hit the hay. I must have died, because I don't remember anything until I felt the day nurse gently shaking my shoulder, telling me to get up and eat breakfast. After breakfast, she dressed my wound, removed the old drain and inserted a new one. While dressing it, she said the doctor would be in about 10:00, and that the ships' stores were on the next level, if I wanted to go up there. I decided to live dangerously and venture forth. Man, this place was like a large department store, on a smaller scale. I moseyed around the place, eye-balling all the goodies, suddenly realizing I didn't have a cent to my name. That sort of took all the joy out of looking, so I returned to the ward and found an old Time Magazine, and caught up on my reading. That's a laugh.

I was still in the magazine when the doctor came in. He was the same doctor who had examined me the day before and sent me down here. We went to his office and he took another look at the opening, prodding around and asking if it hurt or was tender. He replaced the bandage and told me the Hospital Ship, 'Rescue' was weighing anchor today and going to Yokohama, where I would be placed aboard an Army Hospital Ship 'Marigold.' He said there was not much he could do in such a short time, but he did want to talk to me and get the complete story of the operation. For two hours he questioned me as he took notes, after which we had either a long discussion or a bull session, and then he finally took me to lunch, which I assume was an officers mess. He had a meeting to attend and I went back to the ward. I was going through my belonging, wishing I had something to put them in when the nurse, who must have read my mind, walked in with a thermometer in one hand and a sea bag, as she called it, in the other. She took a pulse reading and read the thermometer, then told me we would be moving soon and to let her know if I felt sea sick. She had something for it.

The sea bag was just the thing. It was a blue canvas bag, similar to the small athletic bag you see people carrying into Fitness centers, only not quite as large as some of them. I got all my stuff in nicely and was getting ready to find another magazine to read, when I heard Peggy Lee belting out 'Jealous Heart' on the ship's music system. The nurse called out from her office, asking "You like it?" I gave her the old 'OK' sign as I lay down with magazine and music, thinking I am in heaven again. Such luxury. Another fifteen minutes and we were moving. I must have gone to sleep, for when I awakened, the nurse was bringing me an evening meal.

I read some more and finally turned in about 10:00 p.m. I woke up early, but stayed in bed for some time. When the nurse returned, and I asked her if I could take a bath or a shower. She reached in a closet and handed me a light robe, razor, shaving cream, clean t-shirt and shorts, then showed me the way to the bath, which had tubs and showers. After showering, shaving and putting my dirty underclothes in the hamper, I returned in time for breakfast. The nurse came to pick up the tray, and said we would be docking in another half hour, when someone from the Army would take me to the Army hospital ship. I got another magazine and perused it for another hour. A little after 10.00, two Army Corpsmen with a gurney, rolled into the ward and asked for their patient. After gathering up the starting of my records, the nurse came over to my chair and said they were here. She gave me a big hug and wished me well. The two corpsmen took one look at me, and one asked, "You the POW we are to pick up? You don't look like a POW." I answered him, "And you don't need that gurney, either." With that we had a big laugh and took off. We took an elevator to the dock level and from there we walked a few feet to the shade of a shed, to wait for the ambulance that will take us to the 'Marigold.'

While we were waiting, I watched three or four Japanese working in the shed under the eye of an Army Military Police, or MP. The Japanese are dogging it and the MP knows it, but don't know what to do about it. He says to me. "Look at those lazy SOBs, how do you get them to work?" I asked if he really wants to know, because if he does, he should shout "Kuda, Kuda, Sanyo" and act like you are really pissed off. He wanted to know how I know and what it means. I told him I am an ex-Jap POW and have had it yelled at me for the past three and half years. He asked what the words are again, and in the loudest and gruffest voice, growls out "Kuda, Kuda, Snayo". Those Japs jumped like someone had set a fire under them. The old MP said, "I'll be damn." We jawed a few minutes until the ambulance arrived. When I turned to go, he said, "Thanks, Joe, I wish you could stay around awhile."

We got in the ambulance, me lying on the folded-up gurney, as that was the only place to ride. It was only a short distance down to the dock where the "Marigold" was anchored. Once aboard, I was assigned a ward, and I no more than get settled until I am off for x-rays. Head, chest, lower extremities, legs, feet, arms and hands. From there I. am taken to the lab for blood work, urine specimen and given a plastic jar for a fecal sample the next time I go to the john. After all this, I missed the noon meal, so the nurse went out and brought back the best hamburger I'd eaten in a long time. Several 'dog faces' in the ward are griping because they can't get a hamburger. Anyway, I made the best of what was going to be a difficult situation. The next morning, they sent a gurney in for me, taking me all the way to the upper deck to a stateroom with five double deck bunks. All by my lonesome. Oh well, it is better than listening to the griping down in that ward. By one o'clock I haven't received any lunch and I am beginning to think they have forgotten me, and along about 5:30, still not seeing any chow, I got a little worried because I didn't see or hear anyone. I had a water fountain and a bathroom, but that is all. I am just about ready to go looking for someone, even though they told me not to go wandering around. Finally, just before dark, a couple of women dressed in a peculiar uniform, passed the door. Here is my chance. I ran to the door and, in my loudest, gruffest voice, yelled out "When does a fellow get fed around here?" They turned and stared as if they had seen a ghost. "Who are you?" one of them asked. I told them my predicament. They said they were WACs, but would see what they had good to eat. They asked my name and took off. I thought that was the last I'd see of them. After the first class treatment handed me on the 'Rescue' Navy, I was getting a little disgruntled with the Army.

More people started milling around in the hallways, occasionally looking in and walking on. One even told me that if I moved to the other side, there was a porthole through which I could watch the movie being shown tonight. I told him that was fine, but I had been there since morning and had not had anything to eat. Could he do something about that? "I just work here, Joe." he said. The movie started at dark. I was about to go berserk and tear the place up, when the WACs returned with a Captain who seemed genuinely concerned. He took me down to the officer's mess and arranged to get me something to eat, while he tried to get to the bottom of things.

The administration of a hospital is run on an 8 to 5 basis, with a skeleton crew for night duty. The Captain finally found where I had been admitted, but I was still in the first ward with no record of my having changed wards. He came back and explained what had happened, then took me back to my isolation, promising to return the next morning and see that things got straightened up. With my stomach full and with promises of a better day tomorrow, I moved to the porthole window and watched the remainder of the movie. My WAC friends dropped by to see if things were going well, and wished me a good night, whereupon, I closed the door, turned out the light, and went to sleep. Somewhat disgruntled but feeling I was in better hands than the hands I was in just a few weeks before.

The following morning arrived along with a bountiful breakfast and a visit from a nurse with a cheery "Good morning, Sergeant, and how are we feeling this morning?" At the same time sticking a thermometer in my mouth and taking my pulse rate. When she finished recording her reading, she said this was going to be a busy day for me. First, I had to have more chest x-rays to confirm the findings of the first ones. Then I was scheduled to see an ear, nose and throat doctor; an eye doctor, a dentist, podiatrist, heart and lung doctor and an internist. In between visits, I would be finishing the necessary lab work.

I had barely finished my breakfast when another nurse, along with a WAC and a wheel chair, ushered me out and down to the x-ray department, where four sets of x-ray were made of my chest, front, back and sides. This done in the typical army fashion, hurry up and wait. After maybe an hour or more, I was returned to my isolation cubbyhole. The Red Cross lady dropped by to check if I needed anything, chatted a few minutes and left. This visit was followed by a visit from a WAC with orange juice and some in-between meal snacks. While waiting to be taken to my next appointment, a couple of buddies I knew and had left in the Philippines when I was shipped to Japan, popped in. They had seen my name on a list and wouldn't quit until they were told where I was bunking. A nurse cut that visit short, running them out, telling them if they wanted to visit, to get a mask over their mouth and nose. Which, I should mention, all those who came in wore masks. After all, I had TB, or so they said.

I remained in the ward until after lunch, beginning to believe all those things the nurse told me I would get were not to be. But I was not to be denied. At 2:00 p.m., the technician from the Lab arrived for a blood sample and left a bottle for a urine sample and a folder for a fecal examination, which he said he would pick up in the morning. The remaining afternoon was spent in the dental office and then the optometrist office.

I was returned to my isolated compartment and shortly thereafter, my evening meal was delivered. By this time, I had worked up a pretty good appetite. While I was eating, my buddies returned with their masks and we shot the bull until it was dark and the movie started on the aft deck again. They would have stayed, but there was only one porthole on that side of the room. So they went out on deck to watch the show. We had been joking, while we were shooting the bull, about how a good bottle of San Miguel beer would taste, and they promised to see what they could do about getting one. When the show was over, and the crowd left the area, I was just getting ready to turn in when my buddies popped back in and, believe it or not, had three bottles of Schlitz beer. I don't know how many they had before they came back, but they were feeling no pain. We gulped our beer down pretty fast and they left, because the nurse was due in for her 'before bedtime' rounds. We did not have to worry, because it was almost 10 p.m. before she got to my end of the ship, saying "You have a slight yeasty odor, but I think it will be gone by morning," gave me a big smile and left.

The next three days were more of the same. A lot of hurry up and wait. They would come get me for a 9 o'clock appointment and I would spend the next 30 to 45 minutes sitting in a wheel chair in the hall outside the doctor's door waiting to be called. At least I had a wheelchair to sit in. Others were either standing or sitting on the floor. This went on for three more days, most of the time spent in that little ward by myself. The day before I left, I was taken down to talk to a doctor, who I supposed was a psychiatrist. I had never encountered a psychiatrist before, so I was not prepared for the peculiar questions he asked, or that type of questioning. He was nice enough and made interesting conservation about my experiences, but then here would come one of those odd ball questions or remarks out of left field, that was, to my way of thinking, far from what we had been taking about. I must have passed, because he bade me bon voyage and I left. The next morning, the nurse brought me a large manila envelope. I mean 'large.' It contained all the x-rays taken here on this ship and the end results of all the tests I'd taken. She said I would be leaving sometime during the day, and that I was being flown back to good old USA.

Sixteen of us left the "Marigold" the next day about midmorning, piling into the back of two 2-1/2-ton GI trucks. The trip was uneventful. We must have taken the back roads, and we didn't see much but stark desolation. Upon arrival at Tokyo's largest airport now taken over by the U.S. Air Corps, we were loaded aboard a C-54 converted to a hospital plane for transferring patients faster to the nearest hospital facilities, which were, in this case, the hospital on the island of Saipan. Besides the 16 ambulatory patients that came in trucks, there were several stretcher patients already bedded down when we came aboard. We were assigned narrow bunks along each side of the plane to be our home for the next few hours in flight. There were three nurses, two assigned to the stretcher patients and one to the ambulatory to see that we were belted down for takeoff.

After the plane was in flight we were told we could remove the belts and move about the plane. The nurse broke out some playing cards along with boards for us to lay the cards on for dealing. There were books and magazines for reading, or you could just sit back and relax and/or sleep. Food and drinks were served during the trip. Some of the patients got air sick and stayed in their bunks all the way. I found a book of short stories and read most of them before we got to Saipan.

Ambulances were at the airport to convoy us to the hospital, where we turned in our manila envelopes to a medic while getting in the ambulances which took us to a Quonset hut being used as a ward, and, as no one was there to tell us what to do, we picked out a bed, deposited our belongings on it and proceeded to look the place over. I was getting ready to check out a hallway leading from one hut to the next when a WAC stuck her head in the door and called my name. I thought I was getting in trouble for leaving that hut, but found out that there was someone there to see me. Then I saw three Air Corps officers heading my way. All Captains, no less. The shortest one, Robert Johnston, introduced himself and told me he was the husband of a girlfriend of my sister. He had been asked to be on the lookout for POWs coming through Saipan and had been checking every flight of patients for the past three weeks. He said it might be possible to get me a pass so they could show me around the island. The WAC wasn't sure, but thought it was possible, because it had been done many times since the patients had been arriving on the islands.

Off they went to get the pass, saying they would pick me up later. But such was not to be the case. Not 30 minutes later, a WAC came, telling me to get my gear and come with her. She and another WAC loaded me in the back of a Jeep and hurried me off to purgatory. Isolation again. It was another Quonset hut, but walled off into separate rooms just big enough to take care of a hospital bed and a couple of chairs. I was told to disrobe down to my shorts and t-shirt. At least, this time they explained what the deal was. It seemed the admitting doctor did not concur with the findings of the doctors on the hospital ship, so they were going to run findings of

I Was There, Charley

their own. In the meantime, I was ordered to stay in that room and under no condition could I leave, except go to the john or take a bath. I wasn't about to go anywhere anyway, in my underwear.

My newfound Captain friend found me a couple of days later... he had the pass and a "Guest Card" that entitled me to all the clubs, recreational facilities and just about anywhere something was going on. All for free. I was to be extended any transportation to anywhere I wanted to go. Big deal. Here I was stuck in that isolation ward for what appeared to be the duration. It looked like I might not be able to get out. But those three Captains took good care of me, hauling in everything a body could possible want. So much so that one of the nurses wanted to know whom I knew. I told her if I knew anyone, I would not be there. Those guys came to see me everyday I was there. They were B-29 pilots and had flown many POW food missions. They even brought me some pictures they had taken, and some were of Hirohata, the first Japanese camp I was in. Much later, after I was married and living in Dallas, my sister said that Bob and Betty were stationed at Carswell Field in Ft Worth, and we got in touch with them. They invited us over and we, along with the other two pilots, went out on the town. Bob said they were making good on their offer made years ago on Saipan. Only now one was a Colonel and the other two were Majors. It was like old home week.

Outside of the regular visits by the Captains, the only other excitement happened one morning after I had been there a few days. The Quonset hut next to the one I occupied was the women's Psycho Ward, or so I was told. There was a ten-foot chain link fence around the area, and to the rear of the Quonset hut was a large concrete square block, like maybe an old loading dock. Occasionally, in the morning, before the heat became unbearable, a patient or two would recline on the block and sunbathe. On this particular morning, when I looked out my window, there was a nude woman lying on the concrete block. Suddenly, all hell broke loose. Nurses and WACs appeared out of nowhere, trying to get a robe on her, as she was prancing around like a nymph, daring them to come near her. I could not tell what it was she had in her hand, but it was keeping the nurses and WACs at arms length. Finally, one of the WACs managed to swing the robe and get it entangled in her hands while the others rushed her from each side and rear. She fought them screaming and kicking until they were out of sight. I could still hear her for several minutes, and then all was quiet. Not the best way to start a day, but anything beats nothing.

A couple of days after they put me in the isolation ward, the payroll clerk came round and wanted to know if I wanted some money. He had the payroll made already. It was just a matter of how much I wanted. Here I was with a chance to collect a wad and no way to spend it. He was quite amused by the irony of the situation, but I kept eying that big roll of twenties he had in his hand, and dreaming I figured, drawing Sergeant's rate of pay for three and half years, less a forty dollar allotment I was sending home, I should still have over $3000 coming. So I just, off the top of my head, said, "Gimme a hundred." Real big spender.

On the morning of September 19, Captain Johnston came in for his last visit. He said the whole squadron was flying back to the states that afternoon and he wanted to see if there was anything he could do for me before he left. I told him if he was going home to tell them I was on my way. It looked like it was just a matter of time, and time was the thing I had 'mostest' of at that point in time. Later in the day some of the guys I had come with, came by to tell me they were on their way out the next day. I kept waiting to hear something myself, but they were still hauling me out for more lab tests and interviews. September 21 arrived and another group popped in to tell me they were flying out that afternoon. That was the last notation I made in my diary, so I must have left Saipan on the 22nd or 23rd.

I do remember the day. I had just finished breakfast and was going through my list of literature for something to read that day. After all, there was no radio, no music system, only reading to pass the time. The nurse came in to take my vital signs and, as she was leaving, turned and with a mischievous smile on her face said I would be leaving today. A short time later, a WAC brought my 'Navy issue' clothes in and told me to dress and get my gear together. They

I Was There, Charley

did not waste any time, and 30 minutes later I was in an ambulance headed for the airfield. I was put aboard a C-54 hospital plane with 20 or more patients, several of which were stretcher patients. Most, like me, were ambulatory patients.

One of the nurses told us that we were on our way to good old USA via Johnson Island, Kwajalein, Honolulu and San Francisco. I found out, soon enough, that I was still in isolation. When we landed at both Johnson and Kwajalein, I had to stay on the plane with the stretcher patients. A huge fan was wheeled up to the opening on the plane and air was blown in to keep us reasonably cool in the otherwise tropic heated plane. In flight there was no problem at the altitude we were flying because the air-conditioning was furnished gratis. It was dark when we landed at the Hickam Field in Hawaii. We were all taken to the hospital, where the stretcher patients and I were put in private rooms and fed. I did not know what time it was or what day or what meal I was eating, but I knew I was hungry. All we had on the plane was knick-knacks and soda water. I finished my meal and lay back on the bad. The next thing I knew, someone was shaking me and telling me it was time to go. It was still dark out as we loaded into the ambulance and were taken back to the airbase. As I boarded, one of the nurses said: "Next stop, San Francisco, Soldier. When was the last time you were there?" I told her it had been close to four years.

We were on a different plane, but still a C-54, equipped much the same way as the other. The stretcher patients were evidently left in the hospital in Hawaii. Some new faces were among the group that found bunks and settled in for the night. I awoke to the scent of bacon cooking. What a heavenly smell. By this time we were like the dog who gets up and shakes himself, getting ready for the day, we were shaking ourselves, ready to dive into the source of the sweet-smelling aroma emanating from the kitchen. The remainder of the day, from breakfast until late afternoon, we spent playing card games, reading, shooting the bull and sleeping. About 4 or 4:30 p.m., I became aware of or rather felt, after three previous landings, that we had started the descent. I asked the nurse if we were getting close and she nodded that it wouldn't be long now.

The closer we got and the lower we flew, the more I was overwhelmed by a feeling of complete relief. It was as though I didn't have a care in the world. The tension and suspense of the past three and half years suddenly seemed to evaporate, leaving behind a feeling of euphoria I had never felt before nor have I felt since. As I watched the scenery flash by, and before the wheels hit the concrete of the runway of the air base in Hamilton Beach, California, I thought this is so American. I am home. It seemed to take forever to taxi down the runway to our unloading point. I think you could tell who were the POWs, as they all kissed the good old ground of the United States of America.

We were ushered into the base cafeteria where I saw more food spread out in one place than I had seen in the past three and a half years. Or ever. Maybe a slight exaggeration, but close. To this day I don't remember what I ate that first time back home, but I do remember the sign that said: 'Take all you can eat, but eat all you take.' And I remember the guy in the line in front of me who took eight half-pints of milk. The mess sergeant asked him if he knew what he was doing and the POW said "Just watch me." I guess milk and a steak were two of the most wanted and talked about foods discussed in the bull sessions while we were prisoners. I remember taking a couple of half-pints and going back for a third.

We lingered in the cafeteria for some time before a string of ambulances lined up outside. Each could take three patients, two in the back on stretchers and one in front with the driver. I managed to get a seat with the driver and was able to watch the scenery fly by as we crossed the Golden Gate bridge, our destination being Letterman General Hospital, a short distance from the bridge exit. The POWs were separated from the other patients and taken to different wards, where we were given private rooms and issued the popular hospital maroon jackets and pants. I had given my heavy manila envelope to the nurse in Hawaii and never seen it again. I assumed it came separately on the same plane that brought me. Anyway, my records turned up at Letterman and were reviewed. I had more x-rays, more blood taken and I peed in the bottle again, but I was not put in isolation.

The first thing the personnel arranged for us was a call home. Most of the men made their calls that night. I knew we didn't have a phone in our home and the only way I could get in touch with them was to call the Lumber Yard where my Dad worked. So the next morning after breakfast, considering the time zone difference, I went to the hospital switchboard and had the lady make the call to the Lumber Yard. I talked to Abe Ribble, one of the owners. My Dad was not in at that time, but he called back later when both he and my Mother were on the line. We were concerned about the cost of the call, but the operator told us not to worry, that this one was on Uncle Sam. I told them all I knew about what might happen, but thought I would be going to Bruns General Hospital in Santa Fe, New Mexico, as that was the nearest hospital to my home. With the promise of a visit as soon as possible, we reluctantly hung up.

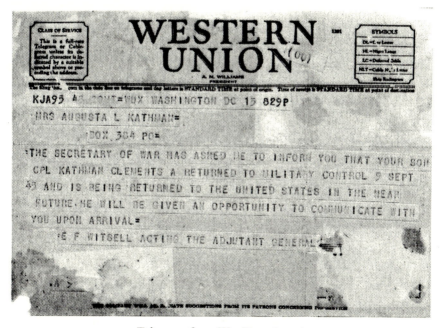

Telegram from War Department

The first two days were mostly taken up with tests, x-rays, etc. On the third day, a nice lady came to the ward and asked the sergeant if there were any patients who would like to take a sight seeing tour of the city. Four of us volunteered…at least we could get out of this place. She had a big, long station wagon. Three of us rode in the back seat and the other one rode up front with her. We all thought this jaunt was to be an hour or two, then back to the hospital, but we were wrong. She began by taking us up to the highest part of the city where you could see for miles in most any direction. The homes up there were out of this world. From there we made the Embarcadero and port area. Part of this, we had seen before shipping out four years earlier. Then we toured the more affluent section of San Francisco, ending up in the driveway of the most gorgeous home I ever had the pleasure of entering. She had made plans for our visit. A sumptuous meal, served by two maids and the lady, a most delightful hostess. After the meal, we were taken on a tour of the house and grounds. This lady obviously had money and I wondered why she would be doing this type thing. As if she was reading my mind, she told us that she had lost a son. A pilot, shot down over the Mediterranean Sea during the North African campaign. "I get so lonely," she said, "when I think about it. You just don't know how good it makes me feel to be around you guys. I love all of you." We spent the rest of the afternoon touring the beach area, taking a long walk with the winds of the Pacific chilling us to the bone since we were only wearing those light hospital jackets. We returned to the hospital in time to make the evening meal, thanking her profusely for her time and hospitality. I have kicked myself many times for not getting her name and address and keeping touch. She was one lovely lady.

We had a Master Sergeant who was attached to our ward. I was never sure of his capacity, but he appeared to pretty much run the place. Since we did not have uniforms, we could not get out of the hospital. We had the run of the grounds, which should have been enough for a bunch of yahoos who'd had no freedom for years, but when it got dark, our feet started to itching to get out and see the night lights. We were setting there one afternoon in my room with the sergeant when the subject came up. He said if we were serious, he thought he could arrange it. With that, he asked our measurements. Only three of us took him up, and within an hour he came back with three sets of uniforms that fit better than what the Quartermaster Corps provided. They had chevrons, service ribbons, unit patches and the works. The only provision was that he go along. He was broke and this small token of our appreciation would suffice for the evening. We each gave him a Twenty Dollar Bill and bought his drinks. We caught a streetcar to what he called his favorite hangout. There were service personnel everywhere. To this day I don't know where we were, and I am glad that sergeant was with us that night. After the third boiler maker (a shot whiskey chased with a bottle of beer,) I don't remember a thing until the next morning when he woke me up to eat my breakfast, telling me that I was leaving soon, on that day. I asked him how I got home, and he said "Why do you think I insisted on going with you guys," then gave me the gory details. I had gone to the john to take a leak and when I didn't return in due time, he went to look in on me and found me passed out, sitting on the stool. No, it's not as you think. I was fully dressed, just sitting there as if I was waiting for a bus. He called a cab and brought me back to the hospital, undressed me and put me to bed. Then went back to take care of the other two. He said they finally got in about 2 a.m. I was so grateful that I gave him another Twenty, cab fare and all. It was worth it to me. But, thinking about it, he was over the barrel because if anything had happened to one of us, his job would have been on the line. With the time he had put in, in the service, he was a career service man and had a lot to lose and only a paltry few Twenty Dollar bills to gain. Man, what a hangover I had, and here I was, taking a flight out.

An hour later I was in an ambulance, this time in the back where I could lay down and rest my aching head. I was not interested in the scenery…I just hoped the driver would keep the bumps to a minimum. Three of us boarded a C-47 along with six or eight more patients, some in stretchers bound for Albuquerque. I found a bunk just outside the door to the pilots area and laid the body down. The nurse came by and strapped me in, then moved on to other patients. She was pretty busy until we landed at the Navy air base near Los Angeles, where two of the stretcher patients were unloaded, then back in the air. When the nurse finally got everyone taken care of and settled down, she sat on the bunk across the aisle from me.

She took one look my way, turned and opened a medicine kit, took out a little white pill and told me she thought I needed it. I took it, asking her what it was. "It's for that hangover," she said, laughing softly as she handed me a paper cup of water to wash it down. "Now lay down and in a little while, you will be feeling one hundred percent better." Sure enough she was right. I never in all of my paths down the booze trail had anything work as well as the little white pill. The trip got a little rough over the Sierra Nevada mountains and several of the patient became air sick and had to hit their bunks. I am usually the first to get seasick, but I had never been airsick and was feeling like a million. The nurse, a Lieutenant, was named Helen Morrison. After playing cards most of the trip she became quite friendly, gave me her address and I gave her mine. I heard from her several times during the 14 months I was at Bruns General Hospital in Santa Fe, New Mexico. Most of the letters were from overseas. She was still ferrying patients around the world. During the summer of 1946, the last letter I got from her, she was engaged to marry a pilot she had met in her many trips around the world.

We arrived in Albuquerque after dark and were met at the airport by many families who had sons as POWs, all hoping the next plane load would be the one that brought their loved one home. One mother of a Sergeant in Battery H was there to see if anyone knew her son. She had been told that he died in O"Donnell POW camp. That Sergeant had been transferred when the 515 CAC unit was formed and I had not seen him after he was captured. I was not aware that he had died. Another POW overheard our conversation and, fortunately, knew all the details of her sons' death.

After most of the visitors left, we were told we would be spending the night in Albuquerque. One lady offered to take us home with her for the night, and some POWs went. We were taken to a mess hall nearby and fed, then to some barracks where we were bedded down for the night. I don't know what they did with the stretcher patients. I was dead tired by this time and slept like a log until aroused the next morning for breakfast. I returned to the barracks, showered and shaved. By the time I had finished, ambulances came to take us to Santa Fe, where I was put in an ambulance and asked if I wanted to lay down or move around. The driver and a medic with my manila envelope rode in the front and I was up and down the whole 60 miles to Santa Fe. That was one long sixty miles. I tried sitting on the end of the stretcher…that wasn't comfortable. I tried laying on my stomach and propping myself with elbows, my hand under my chin…terrible. Finally, I decide to try sleeping. It worked. I should have done it from the start.

We arrived at Bruns around 10 a.m. The ambulance backed up to the rear of the ward and let me out. The WAC waiting at the door was somewhat astonished to see me walk in instead of being carried in. The medic handed her the manila envelope and she asked the medic, "What's in here…lead?" The medic grinned to the driver, "another comedian." With that they were gone, leaving me at my final destination. Not exactly home, but pretty close. Familiar territory, for a change.

Lt. Pauline LaBodie, a spit and polish nurse, was on duty that morning and took care of my admission. The medic had handed some paper to the Guard on the gate when we entered, but the Nurse took care of the admission. She was all business, but oh, so nice. I was given a maroon jacket, pants and white shorts and a t-shirt, and told to remove the clothes I was wearing. I went into the men's rest room and did as I was told, then returned to her office with my clothing, which a WAC put in a bag with my name on it. She assured me it would be laundered and returned to the ward and stored until needed. For the next four months I was on this TB ward with orders not to leave unless in a wheel chair pushed by an attendant. And here I thought I was going home. My family will like that. Pauline said if I needed to make a call to let my family know where I was, to give her the number and she would do it for me. I complied.

The WAC had me follow her and assigned me to a bed just inside the door in a corner. The guy next to me introduced himself, saying, "Welcome to TB row." Man, that damn TB tag has followed me all the way from Japan to the USA. I must be snake bit. Cheer up, man. You got such a short memory that you can forget what it was like just a month or so ago? The WAC returned with a thermometer and proceeded to take my temperature and pulse rate. About this time, the chow wagon came in loaded with trays of food. Two civilian girls busily went about handing out the trays to their respective patients. When they were through, I was the only one without a tray. That figures, I didn't get here early enough to get my name in the pot. So I'll wait till the evening meal. It could be worse. It had been worse.

Not long after the lunch trays were picked up, the nurse came in to tell me she had my Dad on the phone. We had a brief chat and closed by telling me they would probably be up to visit over the weekend. As I was leaving the office the nurse called after me, seemingly very concerned, "You didn't get any lunch did you?" apologizing as she directed me to the small kitchen and told the lady there to fix me anything I wanted while still apologizing. The lady asked me what I would like to eat. The first thing that came to mind was a chocolate malted milk shake, thinking at the same time that was out of the question. But to my surprise, she said: "Your every wish is my command," and set to work making the best chocolate malted ever. She told me to sit down at a table, pulled up a chair and joined me. Her name was Maria and she asked my branch of service and where I had been stationed. When I told her I was a Japanese POW, she immediately wanted to know if I knew so-in-so, who was a cousin. As a matter-of-fact, I knew him well. He had been my truck driver until we had a squabble and the first sergeant transferred him out of my squad. After we moved into Bataan, he was assigned to drive a half-track mobile 75-mm field artillery unit. I had heard rumors their unit had received a direct hit from a 105-mm Japanese field artillery and he was listed as being killed in action, or 'KIO,' but I wasn't sure of the rumor. I just told her I knew him only casually. A few days later his family received the notice that confirmed the rumor. She took a couple of days off and sadly, related the news to me when she returned to work. A little white lie is not always so bad.

True to their word, the following Saturday as I was eating lunch, my whole family paraded into the ward. Mother, Dad, Nelda and Vivian, my two sisters. My brother, Lyle was still in Europe awaiting shipment back to the states. We had a tearful reunion right there before the nurses, WACs and patients. I was told that I would not be able to leave the hospital because I was in a TB ward and all that rot. They stayed a couple of hours, then left to get rooms for the night and visit friends and acquaintances in Santa Fe. We had another long visit Sunday morning before they left. A visit from home, but not home yet.

The next four months were taken up with more x-rays and tests to determine if I had Tuberculosis. I was put on four shots of penicillin a day, to supposedly clear up the infection that was causing the drainage from the incision in my side. Many of the same examinations I had received on the hospital ship and at Letterman Hospital in San Francisco were repeated plus a GI series, kidney x-rays and treatment for five different kinds of intestinal worms, including hookworm. More x-rays of my teeth showed fillings were needed in several teeth. This was competed, as well as another trip to the eye doctor with the good news…I did not need glasses.

After 21 days of penicillin shots, I started developing a rash and itching after each shot. That had me almost climbing the walls, so the shots were discontinued. Anyway, the incision had healed. My sister Nelda and her husband, who had just returned from the Pacific area in time to welcome his new son into the world, came up to see me one weekend, and I was able in talk the doctor into letting me leave the hospital for an overnight visit to get acquainted with my first nephew. While they were here, Captain…now Major Seid, who was also an out-patient at Bruns, invited us to lunch. He and his wife had rented a small house off the post while he was being processed. The Major had visited me regularly after he arrived at the Hospital. One other time he and his wife took me on an extended tour of Santa Fe with a quiet meal at the La Fonda Hotel dining room. They were telling me of their plans to return to the Indian Reservation in Arizona as soon as he was returned to his reserve status. I think that was the last time I saw them. I received a nice gift from them after my wife and I were married and a year or so later some one sent me his obituary notice, clipped from a newspaper. It was a sad note. I felt as if I had lost a member of my immediate family.

With sputum tests every day, x-rays once a month, periodic skin tests and tubes run down my throat into the stomach to siphon off the nightly accumulations, they finally conceded that I did not have Tuberculosis anywhere. So in early February I was given a 30-day leave to go home. HOME! I was finally going home. I caught the first bus out in that general direction. I could not get a bus direct to Portales, New Mexico, some 250 miles away, but had go to Clovis, New Mexico and then transfer to a bus going to El Paso, Texas, which would drop me off in Portales, only 17 miles from Clovis. I called my Dad and had him meet me at the station in Clovis. Six hours later, I departed the bus in Clovis, where my Dad and Vivian were waiting. Another 45 minutes and I was standing in front of 200 E. Center St., Portales, New Mexico. My one-year stint had turned into a mere four years and five months. Four years and five months since I left there on my visit home before being shipped overseas. BACK HOME AT LAST!!!

CHAPTER EIGHT
BACK TO THE HOSPITAL FEBRUARY, 1946--JUNE, 1947

My 30-day leave was cut short by a sudden flare-up of fever. I did not think too much about it at first, because I thought it might simply be from loss of sleep. The nurse I had become quite attached to, and I both had some days off accumulated. She wanted to see the Carlsbad caverns and I told her if she would come to Portales while I was on leave, I would escort her to the caverns. She took me up on my offer, arriving on a Friday and didn't have to be back until the following Tuesday. In my youth, I had a Sunday School Teacher and Scout Leader who was now living in Carlsbad, and we spent the night with him and his wife before visiting the caves. On Saturday morning my sister Nelda, the nurse and I visited Carlsbad, then the caves on Sunday and returned on Monday so she could catch her bus back to Santa Fe on Tuesday. We thought the tour started at 9 a.m., and we had a 20-mile drive to the Cavern site, so we thought we left in plenty time to make the tour, but we missed our bus...the tour started at 8 a.m.

What to do? We drove back to Carlsbad to my friend's home. They were just getting ready to go to church, so we increased the attendance that Sunday by three. After lunch they took us on an afternoon tour of the sights in and about Carlsbad. Carlsbad is on the Pecos River and is quite a picturesque place. We spent another night there, and made the tour Monday. The thought of that long, 180-mile trip back to Portales after the tour was over at 5 p.m. was not pleasant. By the time we returned to Carlsbad and extended our thanks and goodbyes it was nearly 7 p.m. The trip back was long and tiresome, as are all going home trips. We stopped once in Roswell, New Mexico to get gas and something to eat, finally arriving home close to 1 a.m. I had not slept all that well the two nights before and was up early to see the nurse off on the bus, so I thought a good night's sleep would fix me up.

The next morning, my ears were ringing like mad and I felt hot and feverish. I took my temperature and the thermometer read 101. Then it finally dawned on me…this was the way I felt the first time that incision healed before. I immediately checked the groin area on the right side and, sure enough, I could feel the slight bulge. That penicillin did not work. The incision had healed because of the inactivity on the ward. While I was doing the heavy lifting and hard labor, the exertion kept the fluid draining, but when there was no exertion, the fluid did not flow and the incision healed. I told my mother I would have to cut my visit short and get back to the hospital. I still had eight days left, but I was on the first bus out. Back to the hospital!

I arrived back at Bruns around 5 p.m., checked in at the gate and was sent to Ward D-3. I had left C-3, which was the TB ward. D-3 was a surgical ward. When I walked into the office my nurse friend was on duty. "What are you doing back so soon?" she asked. I told her I was running 101 fever and she immediately sat me down in a chair to confirm this. By now, it was 102. She did not exactly panic, but got on the phone and called for a doctor, then proceeded to get me into bed. By this time I was chilling and shaking like a leaf in the wind. The doctor arrived and confirmed the fever. I told him what I thought it was, and after a thorough examination, he confirmed what I thought, ordering something to lower my temperature. He made arrangement for surgery the next morning.

The next morning, bright and early, I was wheeled into surgery, given a spinal anesthesia. I lay there and watched the operation in the reflection of the light reflectors. They opened the cavity, siphoned out the fluid, flushed it out, then stapled the incision shut and brought me back to the ward, still numb from the waist down. By lunch time I was hungry, having missed breakfast. My fever was back to near normal and I ate a hearty meal. I was up and around a couple of days later. As I was not now in a TB ward, I was issued the maroon jacket and pants to wear and could go to the PX.

For the next five or six weeks, I was just bidding my time until they declared me able to be turned to duty, and I could get out of that place. During this time, I became acquainted with one of the men on the enclosed porch attached to the main ward. This was sort of a screened-in affair where there was lots of sunshine and fresh air. My new friend, Stan, was Air Corps and had developed a lung problem while in training in West Texas, and it was aggravated by the humidity and cold in England. He had been transferred to Bruns because it was principally a respiratory hospital. I asked the nurse to be transferred out there when there was an opening. Turnovers were fast, as a rule, and it was only a matter of time until I had a bed on the porch. Stan and I hit it off from the beginning. He had been there for sometime and on his first leave home returned with his Chevrolet two-door sedan. We drove into Santa Fe now and then for a good bowl of Mexican Chili con Carne to break the monotony of the hospital food. We made all the USO dances at the PX annex and in short, lived it up.

That is, until I started to feeling tired and washed out. After a day of so, I told the nurse about it. She took my temperature and I was running a low-grade fever. The doctor checked me out and could not detect anything, so he put me on aspirin to keep the fever down while he ran further tests. My blood showed a high white cell count, which suggested an infection. A couple of days later, while I was showering, I ran the soap bar down through the right groin area and felt a sharp pain. The incision had long healed, so I was sure that was not the problem. I softly probed the area around the incision and felt the sharp pain again. The next morning I told the doctor about it. He took me to the office and had me lower my pants. He gently pressed in that area, shook his head and told me to button up while he called the nurse.

I went back to my bed and a half-hour later here came two medics with a gurney and asked for Sergeant Kathman, then beckoned me to get on the gurney and away we went. I was x-rayed in three or four positions and returned to the ward. Later in the afternoon, the surgeon came in with the x-rays to explain what had happened and what they were going to do about it. The old ruptured appendix was still sloughing off and trying to fill the recently closed cavity. An operation was being scheduled for an appendectomy to remove the ruptured appendix tissue; hopefully, once and for all get me back on my feet and out of there.

This time I was given another spinal anesthesia and was aware of everything that was happening, when suddenly I was racked with pain. The appendix had attached itself to the peritoneum and the ureter, the duct that carries urine from the kidneys to the bladder. According to the doctors, this duct could not be anesthetized. I was then given ether to knock me out, and later sodium pentothal was injected venously to relax me. This I found out some 24 hours later, a lapse of time where I remembered nothing. Those three anaesthetics knocked me for a loop, but after a couple of weeks I was out playing golf, a new game for me.

A new Colonel had taken over the hospital, and a lot of changes were taking place, among which was the treatment of ambulatory patients. They were now required to engage in some stringent exercise for at least thirty minutes a day. The hospital had a large gymnasium and the first day all ambulatory patients gathered there after the doctor's rounds, for 30 minutes of calisthenics. After that, while Stan and I were wandering around the place, we spied some golf bags with clubs. I had never played golf, but Stan was an old hand. While we were checking this out, the Sergeant who had been conducting the exercises, came over and asked if we were golfers. In the course of the conservation we found out we could go to the local 9-hole golf course and play a round of golf and forgo the calisthenics. So that is how I got the golf craze. Stan and I played golf five days a week until we were discharged from the hospital.

The spring and summer, when we were not playing golf, was spent in picnics in the surrounding mountains, sight-seeing in Santa Fe and Taos, in visits to Albuquerque to rodeos and many other events, and as usual, still hanging out at the PX. Several USO shows and USO sponsored dances were held and well attended. It was at one such dance, that I met a young Mexican girl and dated her several times before I was discharged. In the fall of the year the army started closing the hospital and were transferring patients to VA hospitals all over the United States. They were short on personnel to accompany these patients to their varied destinations.

Ambulatory patients were pressed into service. I made one trip with a patient to Wood, Wisconsin Veterans hospital and another two trips to the Hudson VA Center in Jersey City, New Jersey. On both these trips I had long layovers in Chicago and was able to take some short sight seeing trips.

On the trip to New Jersey, after the doctor and I had delivered the patients to the hospital, we had a 60-hour delay in route. He was spending his time in Georgia with his family. I had an old high school buddy that was teaching Spanish in New York City University and I was going to try and look him up, but fate was not with me and my old buddy was in Connecticut for the weekend. So there I was in the big city of New York with nothing to do. As I got off the ferry from Jersey City, I chanced to walk up a street, mainly gawking, and passed a pub. I noticed the long bar with men sitting on stools looking toward the rear. My curiosity aroused, I thought I would check it out. I'd heard about Television, but never expected to see one. Here, before my eyes, were guys all watching the antics of some puppets on TV. I found a stool, ordered a beer and decided to check it out. As I watched and sipped my beer, I became aware of a familiar looking head in front of me. He was in uniform, and when he turned to order another beer, I saw he was a fellow POW from Cabanatuan. I think he was as startled as I was. We had not seen each other in over three years. I knew he was from Dover, New Jersey, but never dreamed I would see him, nor he me. We tried to talk at once and before it was over I was going to spend the next 48 hours as his guest. He had reenlisted and was home on a 30-day leave. It really is a small world. The 48 hours went by rapidly and I was soon on my way back to Santa Fe.

Stan received his transfer orders first. We were trying to get out at about the same time and take a trip out to the west coast and see the sights in California, Oregon and Washington, then take the long trip through the northern states to Chicago and finally to his home in Muncie, Indiana. He got permission to stay around for the next two days until my orders came through. Instead of getting my discharge there at the hospital, I was turned to duty and had to go to San Antonio for reassignment. The best laid plans of mice and men!

We had to change plans. Instead a trip through the scenic west, we chose the Deep South for a trip back to his home.

At Fort Sam Houston I was reassigned and given a TDY, or temporary duty at home until June 1947, at which time I would return to San Antonio for my discharge. We went on to his home via New Orleans, Biloxi, Mississippi; Mobile, Alabama; Pensacola, Florida; Birmingham, Alabama; Atlanta, Georgia; Raleigh, North Carolina; Gauley Bridge, West Virginia; Washington, Pennsylvania; and Muncie Indiana. We had friends in all these places and touched bases with them. I finally got out of Muncie just ahead of a cold front and returned to Amarillo, Texas where I was met by my mother and aunt. I visited my Grandmother for a week or so, and then Mother and I took the bus back to Portales.

For the next six months I was still in the service and drawing my Staff Sergeant's pay. I spent a couple of weeks helping the former advertising manager of the daily newspaper, who had ventured into the field of photography during the war. He had a contract to do the photos for the local college yearbook and was getting farther and farther behind in meeting the deadline. I pitched in and, working 18 hours a day, we finished them off. Record time.

A couple of fellows, one who was my roommate in college, bought a job printing shop in Plainview, but were having a hard time getting quality help. We had all worked in the Texas Tech printing shop, so they sweet talked me into coming to Plainview and helping them until they could find someone or until I received my discharge and moved to Dallas.. So when it came time to return to Fort Ord, I bid them a fond farewell, hooked a ride to Dallas with the photographer friend who was attending a photographer's convention, took a plane to Los Angeles then a train to Ft Ord. The army had closed the separation center at For Sam Houston is why I had to go to California for a discharge.

I arrived at Ft Ord late on a Friday evening. All offices were closed. There were some 15 or 20 of us and I think I was the only one in the group who not reenlisting. We were all put in the same barracks and told we would receive our orders Monday morning.

Come Monday morning, the roll call had me reporting along with the others for an indoctrination session. I tried to get the officers attention, but he told me to see him after the session was over. When I showed him my orders, he apologized and had a sergeant take me to the main office. There I was told my orders would have to be cut again and it would be Wednesday before I could begin to go through the separation process. Three days of hurry up and wait. In the meantime, a case of measles turned up in one of the barracks and they were quarantined for 21 days. The barracks I was in had escaped the quarantine so far. I had just received my discharge and mustering out travel pay and was on my way back to the barracks when I saw the Jeep stop at my barracks. I recognized it by the markings and ran in the back door, grabbed my bags and took off just in the nick of time or I would have been stuck for the next 21 days in that barracks. I caught a truck going in to Salinas, then a bus to Las Angeles, riding all night and arriving just in time to grab the old Santa Fe milk train for points east to New Mexico. Three days later, after sitting in a chair car and trying to sleep because there were no Pullmans available, I made it back to Clovis, New Mexico. I walked down Highway #70 going to Portales and points south, thumbed a ride and, twenty minutes later, I was back home and finally, FREE!

EPILOGUE

A few months after being admitted to Bruns Hospital, I met LaVerne Gensler, a WAC who was the NCO in charge of the X-Ray and Laboratory section. We both loved to dance and were in the Enlisted Men's Club almost every night. My friend Stan was dating a nurse from Pennsylvania, so we double dated most of the spring and summer of 1946 and when LaVerne was discharged, I saw her off on the bus to Dallas, Texas. We corresponded regularly and when I was working in Plainview, Texas, I went to Dallas almost every weekend. We became engaged and were married on August 19, 1947. Five years and three miscarriages later, on December 27, 1952, Clemens A. Kathman III was born.

I moved to Dallas in July of 1947 and was employed by the Dallas Times Herald where I worked for thirty-five years, during which time I saw the printing business move from the old hot metal process of printing to the computer age of photocomposition, and I grew along with it, also working part time in the electronic industry servicing radios, music systems, televisions, videos, industrial electronics and micro-electronics. I retired from both businesses at the same time, December 16, 1981.

For the first few years, my son was highly allergenic and suffered from asthma and eczema. In spite of his handicap, he was an honor student in Junior High and High School, graduating cum laude from Abilene Christian College. He is married and has three children, Jason, now a senior at Texas Tech, with a 3.5 grade point average; Kimmy, a sophomore at Texas Tech with a 3.5 grade point average, and Jon Ryan, who will be a freshman in Coppell High School next year and is a straight A student.

After forty-two years of marriage and a two-year battle with emphysema, LaVerne died on January 5, 1987. I then married Mary Wilkinson in February 1988, gaining not only a wife but several step children and even step grandchildren. Mary died from heart and lung problems after only four years of marriage. I tried bachelorhood for ten years, then married Margaret Jenkins from Brenham, Texas on July 22, 2002, in Las Vegas, Nevada.

I found time, during my years of bachelorhood, to become active in Freemasonry, a fraternity dear to my heart. I was able to go through the chairs and serve as Master of my lodge, the R.C. Buckner Lodge #1176 AF & AM, serving as High Priest of the Seagoville Chapter and thrice Illustrious Master of the Seagoville Council of the York Rite of Freemasonry. I was invested a Knight Commander of the Court of Honor in the Scottish Rite of Freemasonry in 1993, Coroneted a 33 degree Honorary Inspector General in the Scottish Rite of Freemasonry in 1999. Made a full member of the Texas Lodge of Research after presenting, having read and published an article about Freemasonry. Served as editor of the Grotto Newsletter for nine years, served faithfully as an Outer Guard of Hella Shrine for eight years, served as Senior Steward of Dallas Lodge #760 for two years, and was Food Coordinator of the Dallas Valley of Scottish Rite of Freemasonry for six years, working as parking lot supervisor the last four years, for a total of nine years. I am also an Endowed member of Tranquility Lodge #2000, a life member of the Scottish Rite Research Society, a member of Portales Lodge #26 AF & AM, Portales, New Mexico, as well as the Southern California Lodge of Research, Audie L. Murphy Chapter of National Sojourners and the Royal Order of Scotland.

I am 87 years young and recently joined the Brenham, Texas Lodge of the Sons of Hermann along with my wife, who is to blame for grammatical errors in this book. We count ourselves fortunate and blessed by God to have so much, and to live in the good old U.S.A.

Printed in the United States
26011LVS00003B/577-600